HABERMAS, MODERNITY AND LAW

PHILOSOPHY & SOCIAL CRITICISM

Series Editor: David M. Rasmussen, Boston College

This series presents an interdisciplinary range of theory and critique emphasizing the interrelation of continental and Anglo-American scholarship as it affects contemporary discourses. Books in the series are aimed at an international audience, focusing on contemporary debates in philosophy and ethics, politics and social theory, feminism, law, critical theory, postmodernism and hermeneutics.

Other books in this series
David Owen, *Nietzsche, Politics and Modernity*
Richard Kearney (ed.), *Paul Ricoeur: The Hermeneutics of Action*
Nick Crossley, *Intersubjectivity: The Fabric of Social Becoming*

HABERMAS, MODERNITY AND LAW

EDITED BY
Mathieu Deflem

SAGE Publications
London • Thousand Oaks • New Delhi

© Sage Publications 1996

This edition first published 1996

Previously published as a Special Issue of the journal
Philosophy and Social Criticism, volume 20 (1994),
number 4.

SAGE Publications Ltd
6 Bonhill Street
London EC2A 4PU

SAGE Publications Inc
2455 Teller Road
Thousand Oaks, California 91320

SAGE Publications India Pvt Ltd
32, M-Block Market
Greater Kailash - I
New Delhi 110 048

British Library Cataloguing in Publication data

A catalogue record for this book
is available from the British Library

ISBN 0 7619 5136 9
ISBN 0 7619 5137 7 (pbk)

Library of Congress catalog record available

Typeset by Type Study, Scarborough, North Yorkshire
Printed in Great Britain by The Cromwell Press Ltd,
Broughton Gifford, Melksham, Wiltshire

Contents

Mathieu Deflem

Introduction: law in Habermas's theory of communicative action

The papers in this collection present themes of discussion pertinent to law and legal processes raised by the perspective of Jürgen Habermas's theory of communicative action. Habermas's writings are widely acclaimed among the major contributions to the theoretical understanding of contemporary society, and specifically his legal theory has since recent years become a topic of growing scholarly attention. However, to date, the debate on Habermas and law has largely been confined to a predominantly European audience of specialists in the tradition of Critical Theory, and most discussions have taken place in moral and legal philosophy rather than in empirically oriented studies of law.[1] Given the growing concern in the field of legal studies to interconnect broad philosophical and theoretical perspectives with empirically based research on specific social issues – an aspiration which is in fact central to Habermas's work – the contributions in this book hope to fulfill a twofold purpose.

First, this collection seeks to acquaint legal scholars, in the broadest sense of the term, who are as yet not familiar with Habermas's perspective, with an innovative contribution to the study of modern societies, specifically concerning issues and problems of law. This volume hopes to provide insights that clarify Habermas's theory of society and its approach to law, discuss some of its values and limitations, and suggest ways in which Habermas's work may contribute to the theoretical understanding as well as the empirical investigation of law and law-related processes.

Second, the papers in this book represent a range of different scientific disciplines, bringing forth a varied set of concerns and positions. The diversity of perspectives and discussion themes will hopefully enable readers to gain access not only to the broad scope that characterizes Habermas's writings, but also to some current approaches to law which are inspired by his work. In this respect, the papers present several avenues and issues of interest to the legal scholarship, including discussions of Habermas's work from its initial formulation up to its most recent developments.

To ease comprehension of the overall theoretical framework which the papers build on, I will in this introduction briefly outline the main tenets of Habermas's theory of communicative action. I limit this presentation of Habermas's approach to law and society to the formulation in *The Theory of Communicative Action* and its developments until the publication of *Faktizität und Geltung*.

With his two-volume work *The Theory of Communicative Action* (1984, 1987a), Habermas has undoubtedly formulated an innovative and influential theory of society, but the book (as are most of Habermas's writings) is by all standards not easy to read. In particular, the structure of argumentation, which seeks to develop a social theory on the basis of detailed, meta-theoretical discussions of a wide range of classical and contemporary social theories, may initially discourage potential readers from a thorough investigation of the work.[2] A brief presentation of Habermas's general theoretical framework, therefore, may help to clarify his approach to law as well as some of the criticisms which have thus far been suggested in the literature. This review will also situate the discussions of Habermas's legal theory presented in the papers in this book.

I The theory of communicative action: concepts and theses

Habermas's theory of communicative action fundamentally rests on a distinction between two concepts of rationality that shape knowledge to guide action (Habermas, 1984: 8–22, 168–85). First, cognitive-instrumental rationality conducts action that aims at the successful realization of privately defined goals. These action types are either instrumental, when they are directed at efficient interventions in a state of affairs in the world (e.g. through labor), or strategic, when they guide attempts to successfully influence the decisions of other actors (e.g. in relations of domination). Second, communicative rationality underlies action that is aimed at mutual understanding, conceived as a process of reaching agreement between speaking subjects to harmonize their interpretations of the world. To avoid misunderstanding, it is important to note that Habermas's concept of communicative action does not assume that subjects can aim at mutual understanding only through speech-acts (i.e. language as it is used in interaction between at least two actors), or that agreement would, as an innocent prefiguration in thought, be the necessary outcome of all communicative processes. Several forms of action that are not linguistic (signs, symbols) can also be oriented to understanding, but only if they can be transferred into interactions mediated through language. Also, communicative actors' orientation to agreement does not exclude the possibility of dissent as the result of distorted or unresolved communication. Habermas maintains that it is only through language, under conditions of rational argumentation, that social actors can coordinate their actions in terms of an orientation to mutual understanding.

Habermas analyzes the conditions of rational argumentation in communicative action on the basis of a distinction between different validity claims that are implicitly or explicitly raised in speech-acts. He distinguishes the following validity claims: comprehensible and well-formed speech-acts make an objective claim to truth, a normative claim to rightness, and expressive and evaluative claims to authenticity and sincerity (Habermas, 1984: 319–28). Different types of discourse serve to explicitly address these claims: theoretical discourse on truth; moral-practical discourse on normative rightness; and aesthetic and therapeutic critique on authenticity and sincerity (Habermas, 1984: 22–42). On the basis of this theory of argumentation, Habermas develops the two-level approach of lifeworld and system.

The claims of communicative actions in everyday social life, Habermas argues, are often not questioned or criticized because they are raised within the contours of an undisputed, shared lifeworld (Habermas, 1987a: 119–52). The lifeworld offers the commonly accepted background knowledge within which action can be coordinated. Characteristic for the rationalization of occidental societies is that the lifeworld has differentiated along the lines of the validity claims of speech-acts. Thus, a differentiation into three performative attitudes in communicative action has been brought about: an objectivating attitude towards the outer world of events and circumstances, a normative attitude towards the social world of a community of people, and an expressive attitude towards the inner world of the subjectivity of the individual. Habermas's concept of the lifeworld is therefore not limited to the cultural tradition (the shared interpretations of the world) of a particular community. Next to providing a set of cultural values, the lifeworld also secures that social actors abide by the normative standards of their society (for the solidarity of social groupings), and that social actors are enabled to act as competent personalities in harmony with their social environment (identity formation).

Three structural components of the lifeworld correspond to these functions: culture, society and personality. At the level of culture, cultural reproduction relates to the transmission of interpretation schemes consensually shared by the members of a lifeworld. At the level of social interaction, social integration refers to the legitimate ordering of interpersonal relations through the coordination of actions via intersubjectively shared norms. Finally, at the level of personality, socialization processes seek to ensure that personalities with interactive capabilities are formed. Culture, society and personality are the structural components of the rationalized lifeworld. Thereby, the process of societal rationalization entails a differentiation of a once unified lifeworld into different structural domains and specialized social institutions. The lifeworld, then, has a twofold meaning: on the one hand, the horizon-forming contexts of culture, society and personality within which communicative action takes place, and, on the other hand, the resources of possibilities from which participants in communicative action can transmit and renew cultural knowledge, establish solidarity and build social identity.

Habermas's theory of social evolution takes an important turn when he argues that the action-oriented approach of the lifeworld cannot account for all the complexities of modern societies. The process of rationalization should be understood not only as a differentiation of the lifeworld as a symbolically reproduced communicative order, but also in terms of the 'material substratum' of society (Habermas, 1987a: 235–82). This twofold perspective indicates that societies have to secure the transmission of cultural values, legitimate norms and socialization processes, and, in addition, they also have to efficiently manipulate and control their environment in terms of successful interventions. Habermas therefore supplements the perspective of the lifeworld with a systems theory, specifically paying attention to the economic and the political system (Habermas, 1987a: 338–43). These systems have in the course of history split off, or 'uncoupled', from the lifeworld to function independently, no longer on the basis of communicative action aimed at understanding, but in terms of the functionality of the steering of media, money and power. Actions coordinated through these steering media relieve communicative action from difficulties in reaching consensus in complex societies characterized by a range of action alternatives and, therefore, a constant threat of dissent. Actions coordinated by the steering media of money and power differ from communicative action in that they aim at the successful (cognitive-instrumental) organization of the production and exchange of goods on the basis of monetary profit (economy) and the formation of government to reach binding decisions in terms of bureaucratic efficiency (politics).

Habermas does not conceive the 'uncoupling' of system and lifeworld as problematic in itself. The coordination of action in systems can best be secured by steering media because they manage to relieve communicative actions from the possibility of dissent, and they can do so with a high level of productivity and efficiency. However, systems also have the capacity to penetrate back into the lifeworld. Coordination mechanisms oriented to success thereby enter into the domains of the lifeworld (culture, society and personality) that should be secured through communicative action oriented to mutual understanding if they are to remain free from disturbances and crisis manifestations (Habermas, 1987a: 318–31). This process Habermas refers to as the colonization of the lifeworld: the communicative potentials aimed at understanding in the lifeworld are eroded in terms of the systemic imperatives of monetary and bureaucratic systems interventions.

II Lifeworld, system, and the rationalization of law

In *The Theory of Communicative Action*, Habermas develops an approach to law based on a discussion of two important developments in the process of societal rationalization. First, the separation of law from morality is crucial for the differentiation of system and lifeworld, and, second, legal processes help explain current manifestations of the systems colonization of the lifeworld in western societies.

1 Law and the differentiation of system and lifeworld

Habermas attributes to law the important role of normatively 'anchoring' or institutionalizing the independent functioning of the steering media of money and power. The legal norming of money and power is central in bringing about the uncoupling of the economic and political systems from the lifeworld (Habermas, 1987a: 164–97, 264–82). Historically, the differentiation of the political system first occurred when political authority crystallized around judicial positions holding the means of force. Further processes of separation between political offices increased the complexity of political organization which fully matured in the modern state. In the framework of societies organized around the state, markets arose that were steered by the medium of money. Relieved from the indeterminacy of communicative action, the political system of the modern state set collective goals reached through binding decisions in terms of power, while the economy secured the production and distribution of goods in terms of monetary productivity. These systems are 'formally organized domains of action ... that – in the final analysis – are no longer integrated through the mechanism of mutual understanding, that sheer off from lifeworld contexts and congeal into a kind of norm-free sociality' (Habermas, 1987a: 307).

To bring about this uncoupling of system and lifeworld, Habermas argues, law has to institutionalize the independence of economy and state from lifeworld structures (Habermas, 1987a: 164–79). Law is the institution that establishes the normative 'anchoring' of the steering media of money and power in the lifeworld. In other words, systems can operate independently from the lifeworld only when they are recoupled to the lifeworld through the legalization of their respective media. In the case of the money medium, exchange relations have to be regulated in property and contract laws, while the power medium of the political system needs to be normatively anchored by institutionalizing the organization of official positions in bureaucracies. Therefore, the differentiation of systems requires a sufficient level of rationalization of the lifeworld through a separation of law and morality, and of private and public law. The separation of law and morality is achieved at the post-conventional level of social evolution, i.e. when legal and moral representations are based on abstract principles that can be criticized, rather than on specific values that are directly tied up to concrete ethical traditions. Morality then becomes a personal matter of concrete but subjective moral-practical concerns, while law, as a social institution with external force, materializes abstract normative standards for the whole of society. The separation of private and public law corresponds to the independent functioning of the economy (e.g. contract law) and politics (e.g. tax law).

The underlying viewpoint of Habermas's discussion of law as the normative legalization of the independent functioning of systems is that law can formally be conceived as an institutionalization of practical discourse on social norms (Habermas, 1984: 243–71). Habermas acknowledges (with Weber) that modern law in western societies is positive (expressing the will of a sovereign lawgiver), legalistic (applying to deviations from norms) and formal (what is not legally forbidden is allowed). In this sense, modern law is positivized into a functional, technical system that seems to have suspended any need for moral deliberation. However (and contrary to Weber's view), Habermas argues that law at the post-conventional level of social evolution is still based on moral principles which remain open to discussion: 'The particular accomplishment of the positivization of the legal order consists in *displacing* problems of justification, that is, in relieving the technical administration of the law of such problems over broad expanses – but not in doing away with them' (Habermas, 1984: 261). Modern law as a whole remains in need of justification, and can be criticized, precisely in order to unveil its systemic nature, under the abstract conditions of universalistic validity claims on normative rightness.

2 Law, juridification and the colonization of the lifeworld

The second important role Habermas assigns to law from the perspective of the theory of communicative action concerns the thesis of the internal colonization of the lifeworld (Habermas, 1987a: 356–73). Habermas develops this thesis in a discussion of the processes of juridification in the course of (European) history. The concept of juridification generally refers to an increase in formal law in the following ways: the expansion of positive law, i.e. more social relations become legally regulated; and the densification of law, i.e. legal regulations become more detailed. Habermas identifies four waves of juridification in the specific context of European welfare states.

The first wave of juridification took place during the formation of the absolutist bourgeois state in Europe. The sovereign's monopoly over force, and the contractual rights and obligations of private persons, were regulated to legitimize the coexistence of a strong monarchical state and a market of free enterprise. Second, the bourgeois constitutional state of the 19th century gradually regulated individual rights against the political authority of the monarch: life, liberty and property of private subjects were constitutionally guaranteed. Next, with the creation of the democratic constitutional state in the wake of the French Revolution, citizens' social rights to participate in the formation of the political order were regulated to democratize the power of the state. Finally, with the rise of the social welfare state of the 20th century, the economic system of capitalism was for the first time bridled through legislation securing individual freedoms and social rights over and against the imperatives of the free market.

The three last juridification tendencies, Habermas argues, indicate how lifeworld demands attempt to resist the autonomous workings of state and economy. This is achieved first by claiming individual rights against the sovereign, then by democratizing the political order, and finally by guaranteeing freedoms and rights against the economic system. Habermas claims that the present form of juridification in welfare states is nevertheless markedly ambivalent because each freedom guaranteed at once means a freedom taken away. Habermas discusses four central problems of social-welfare laws that explain this ambivalence: (1) the formal restructuring of legal interventions in the lifeworld entails an *individualization* of legal claims; (2) the conditions under which social laws apply are *formally* specified; (3) legal entitlements relate to social problems but are *bureaucratically* implemented through centralized and computerized impersonal organizations; and (4) social-welfare claims are often settled in the form of *monetary* compensations (the consumerist redefinition). The demands of the lifeworld, then, are thereby transformed into imperatives of bureaucratic and monetary organizations, so that law comes to intervene in a systemic way into the social relations of everyday life. When legal regulations are observed to conform to the imperatives of state and economy, the lifeworld is also colonized, internally, by the law as medium.

Habermas claims that the law as medium remains bound up to the law as the institutionalized domain of practical discourse. The law as medium applies to the legal organization of economy and state, as well as to the interventions of welfare policy regulations in the informal structures of the lifeworld. As instances of the latter case, Habermas mentions school and family laws that manage to convert contexts of social integration over to the medium of law in terms of bureaucratic and monetary controls. These laws do not need any substantive justification but are simply a matter of functional procedure. Law as an institution, on the other hand, retains an intimate connection with morality. Legal institutions, such as constitutional and criminal law, refer to regulations that have to be normatively evaluated, and that remain in need of justification in terms of moral-practical discourse.

III Some problems and prospects of Habermas's legal theory

Habermas's observations on law have inspired theory and research on law and legal processes, leading to some interesting insights on the theoretical and empirical strengths and limitations of Habermas's approach. I will briefly review the main issues that these critical discussions and applications have dealt with, and specifically address some of the topics that are debated in this volume's papers.

The theme which has inspired most debate in relation to Habermas's conception of law is his formulation of the ethics of discourse.[3] With this moral-philosophical proposition, Habermas has explicated how the procedural conception of morality can be conceived. In *The*

Theory of Communicative Action, Habermas argues that modern law, rather than having rationalized into a completely functional entity, remains in need of moral justification in terms of a practical discourse on the rightness of norms. The question, then, is how this discourse can be conceived to assure rational argumentation? Habermas argues that from a post-metaphysical perspective, philosophy can no longer pretend to offer undisputed, rationally justified, right moral norms (as the substantive foundation of legal norms). Rather, philosophical investigations can at best outline the rational conditions of the procedure under which norms can, and should, be grounded by people in the context of their lifeworlds. The principle of the ethics of discourse therefore states: 'Only those norms can claim to be valid that meet (or could meet) with the approval of all affected in their capacity *as participants in a practical discourse*' (Habermas, 1990a: 66). While Habermas realizes that any such discourse on norms can only unfold within the boundaries of specific ethical lifeforms, he nevertheless maintains that the suggested principle is strictly procedural and in this sense universally applicable.

Discussions on Habermas's ethics of discourse have mostly concerned its procedural status, rather than its association with law. Some authors, for instance, have argued that Habermas's moral philosophy does in fact contain substantive values.[4] Notions of democracy, autonomy and equality are taken up in Habermas's theory, but only implicitly, which may have led him to underestimate the possibly distorting influence of concrete lifeforms in which practical discourse can take place. On the other hand, it has also been suggested that Habermas does not develop a true moral theory, and that his formalistic proposition is normatively 'empty'.[5] The ethics of discourse, it is argued, is an indecisive methodology that does not provide any substantive moral principles and fails to formulate the road to an ideal society. A meaningful application of the discourse principle can at best be achieved through implementing and investigating procedural requirements inasmuch as they fulfill the realization of substantive principles of human rights, solidarity, care, freedom, or justice.

The proposition that Habermas's procedural ethics of discourse should be expanded with substantive norms has also been taken up in some legal research inspired by the theory of communicative action. Notably the German legal theorist Robert Alexy (1989a; 1989b; 1990) has applied Habermas's discourse theory to an analysis of law, and suggested that an application of the model of practical discourse to legal discourse is in any case contextualized by the concrete norms that are already present in any given legal structure. Thus, law always constitutes a substantive ethics to which analyses in terms of the discourse model are subordinate. Legal research on the basis of the ethics of discourse, therefore, should take into account principles that are more fundamental than, and can serve as a standard to confront, normative claims in courts of law. This would permit the laying bare, and criticizing, of the underlying normative principles that guide legal processes of, for instance, constitutional law and legal procedure. Finally, in line with the critique of the indecisive nature of the ethics of discourse, it has been advanced that legal research in terms of Habermas's discourse ethics only makes sense if law is subjected to a critique in terms of procedural requirements inasmuch as they meet, or fail to meet, substantive normative principles. Particularly, human rights, far from being taken for granted, should be confronted with legal procedures.

The relevance of the procedural notion of morality has also been of concern in the debate between Habermas and the Critical Legal Studies (CLS) movement.[6] While analyses from the CLS perspective share with Habermas the view that law and morality are closely related, CLS scholars have generally argued against the possibility of rationally reconstructing law's moral grounding in terms of a universal procedure of discourse. The moral justification of law is denied in favor of a demystification of legal morality and decision-making as an arbitrary 'patchwork quilt'. Habermas has responded to this position by arguing that, while CLS scholars perform a valuable task in criticizing the functions of law in terms of its own aspirations, they fail to offer any justification or rational basis for their criticism. They thereby confront the paradox of implicitly presupposing a rational standard to substantiate their own moral position, at the same time questioning the possibility of its existence in law.[7]

The question of the moral foundations of law (or the extent of differentiation of law from morality) is also the central issue that sets Habermas's work most clearly against the legal theory of Niklas Luhmann.[8] Luhmann suggests that societal evolution has reached such a high level of differentiation in modern societies that law is an autopoietic system which no longer needs any justification in terms of normative points of view. The autopoietic perspective of law implies that the legal system is operationally closed so that it functions only in terms of its own binary code (lawful/unlawful) set in its own programs (laws). Other social systems, including morality, are in like manner closed, and while exchange of information between different systems is possible, the intransparency between systems prevents interference of any one system in the autonomous operation of another. Hence Luhmann argues that law cannot and does not need to be morally grounded to secure its internal functionality.

Obviously, Luhmann's perspective is in marked contrast to Habermas's conception of law, specifically on the question of the moral justification of law. On the basis of the two-level perspective of system and lifeworld, Habermas interprets processes of juridification as the ambiguous result of lifeworld resistances transformed in terms of the imperatives of the political and the economic system. Whereas monetary and bureaucratic interventions in law can be conceived in terms of purposive functionality, the lifeworld dimensions of law, Habermas maintains, should be analyzed from the perspective of communicative action aimed at mutual understanding. Habermas's identification of law as an institution, which is still in need of moral justification, and law as a medium, as a system detached from moral-practical concerns, precisely points out the central 'ambiguity in the rationalization of law' (Habermas, 1984: 270).

This debate raises a final issue pertinent to explore in relation to Habermas's legal theory, and to which his most recent works on law have paid much attention. It concerns the relationship between the functionality of law (as a medium) and its continued need for moral justification (as an institution). This problem stems from the fact that in *The Theory of Communicative Action*, Habermas attributed a crucial, yet somewhat ambivalent, role to law in the evolution of modern societies.[9] As an institution, law is linked to morality and as such part of the lifeworld, while as a medium, law is a functional entity just like the political and economic systems. The ambiguity in this formulation is that it seems to rigidly separate two types of law: some laws make a claim to normative rightness and are open to critique, while others are purely a matter of systems imperatives (in terms of efficiency and productivity). In addition, Habermas originally argued that law as a medium remains bound to law as an institution, and yet, they follow quite different paths of rationalization (cognitive-instrumental versus communicative). The thesis of juridification and internal colonization of the lifeworld, then, seems to neglect the possibility that law as an institutional complex of the lifeworld can be restructured by systems to bring about a colonization of law, rather than that law is itself a colonizing medium. This formulation would allow for a position that retains law's intimate connection to morality, while not denying the possibility of systems imperatives intervening in law. Indeed, Habermas argues in some of his most recent publications that modern law is situated between lifeworld and system because, and to the extent that, law is rational in terms of the just procedures of law established and secured in democratic constitutional states.[10] In other words, modern law, while not free from possible interferences by the formally organized systems of politics and economy, can be morally grounded. Law can be legitimate in terms of moral-practical discourse, not because it incorporates concrete, ethically right values, but because it relies on a procedurally conceived notion of rationality realized by democratic principles in legislation, jurisprudence and legal administration.

IV An overview of the contributions

The question of the legitimacy of law, with which I ended my review of the debate on Habermas's legal theory, has occupied center stage in Habermas's latest writings on law. As I noted, the rigidly drawn distinction between the functionality and the morality of law made it problematic to retain the notion of the internal colonization of the lifeworld while at the same time holding on to the argument that law as a whole remains in need of moral justification. These considerations on the necessity and possibility of the legitimacy of legality led Habermas to the negative conclusion that he 'cannot maintain the distinction [he] made in the second volume of *The Theory of Communicative Action* between law as a medium and law as an institution' (Habermas, 1990b: 130). With the recent publication of *Faktizität und Geltung* (Habermas, 1992a; forthcoming as *Between Facts and Norms*), Habermas has thoroughly addressed this theme and elaborately dealt with the legitimacy of law, specifically in the context of democratic constitutional states. In conformity with this perspective, the issue of legitimate or valid law constitutes the unifying theme of the discussions in this book.

In his review of *Faktizität und Geltung*, David Rasmussen usefully locates the critical themes of Habermas's most recent explorations in legal theory. Habermas's *Faktizität und Geltung* will no doubt spark an extensive debate on the possibility of legitimate law. The fact that within a year of its original publication the book has already enjoyed four German editions testifies to this. Yet the work is of considerable complexity so that a brief review of its main theses may serve as a helpful introduction. Beyond this, Rasmussen with clarity situates Habermas's central concern with the normative validity of law within the general context of his theory of communicative action, as well as within a wider tradition of legal philosophy and sociology of law. In fact, the differentiation between the philosophy and the sociology of law – or the transformation from Hegel to Weber – serves as a vehicle for the elaboration of Habermas's treatise on the facticity and validity of law. This crucial duality, Rasmussen argues, in turn exemplifies the uniqueness of Habermas's perspective, specifically in the context of liberal societies, and its position vis-a-vis other legal traditions, ranging from Rawls, Dworkin and legal hermeneutics, to Critical Legal Studies, legal realism and Luhmann.

Pierre Guibentif's paper also, but from a different perspective, addresses the duality of law – philosophical and sociological, or ideal and real. In a bridge-building exercise not uncharacteristic for Habermas's perspective, Guibentif explores the production of law as an avenue for the cross-fertilization between legal approaches from the standpoint of the elucidation of legal legitimacy, on the one hand, and an interactionist perspective of social forces shaping the reality of law, on the other. He thereby traces the evolution of Habermas's legal theory from its earlier formulation on the connection between theory and practice, and its ramifications for political and legal philosophy, to the linguistic turn of the theory of communicative action and the centrality of the validity question.

In his essay on human rights and criminal procedure, Peter Bal tackles the problem of the relation between law and morality in confrontation with an application of Habermas's ethics of discourse to legal procedures. As I noted above, the problem of formalism versus implicit substantivism is arguably the most debated question on Habermas's moral philosophy, and Bal, from one side of the debate, examines its implications for the field of criminal law. In court cases on criminal matters, the discursive claims to moral rightness occupy a central place, and they offer an important site for an application of Habermas's theory of argumentation. Yet, Habermas's procedural model, Bal argues, needs to be elaborated by human rights as the substantive content or ultimate standard by which the legitimacy of legal decisions can be determined.

Bernhard Peters, finally, engages in a reconstructive attempt to trace the duality of law from a confrontation between internal or meaning-oriented approaches and external or systems-theoretical perspectives. Within this confrontation, in which is recognized Habermas's perspective of lifeworld and system, Peters opts for a reconstructive perspective that analyzes from the participants' point of view the meaning, aspired and actual, of law. Peters discusses how Habermas recently formulated the possibility of this reconstruction, and argues that the institutional guarantees through a realization of democratic procedures ('collective freedom') that Habermas suggests narrowly center on procedural requirements at the expense of substantive appeals made to certain rights and principles. Turning to an empirically founded approach to law, Peters adds that the distinction which Habermas draws between lifeworld and system, and the conflation of normative and empirical theorizing that accompanies it, in fact lead to an unjustifiable reified dualism. Therefore, Peters proposes an analytical approach that seeks to uncover law as a complex involving intentional as well as non-intentional mechanisms and processes.

Acknowledgments

Earlier versions of the papers here published were first presented at the annual meeting of the Law and Society Association in Philadelphia, May 1992. I thank the participants and discussants at the meeting sessions for their stimulating contributions and lively discussions. Thanks are likewise due to Austin Sarat who, as chair of the program committee, assisted with the preparations of the sessions, and to Gary T. Marx, member of the Philadelphia organizing committee, at whose recommendation the sessions were organized. I acknowledge gratitude to Professor Habermas who, though not present at the meeting, kindly agreed to participate in the debate in the form of his 'Postscript' to the fourth edition of *Faktizität und Geltung* (1994), which we here offer in English translation. I am grateful, finally, to Lawrence Cohen, Thomas McCarthy, Heide Natkin, David Rasmussen, William Rehg, and Ros Spry and Jane Makoff at Sage Publications, for their valuable help in preparing this book.

University of Colorado, Boulder

Notes

I thank Eve Darian-Smith and Gary T. Marx for their comments on a previous version of this introduction.

1   This is not to suggest that Habermas's theories have not received attention in the field of legal studies outside Europe's borders. For general introductions and critical reviews of Habermas's approach to law, for instance, see: Brand (1987); Eder (1988); Haarscher (1986); Murphy (1989); Preuss (1989); Raes (1986); Scheuerman (1993); van der Burg (1990). Habermas's theory has meanwhile also found its way into empirical research in the American law and society tradition, dealing with such diverse issues as feminist legal thought (Cole, 1985), environmental law (Northey, 1988), legal interpretation (Hoy, 1985;

Mootz, 1988), professional roles in the legal community (Dan-Cohen, 1989), and analyses of legislation and constitutional regulations (Feldman, 1993; Felts and Fields, 1988; Leedes, 1991; Solum, 1989). For further references, see the Bibliography in this book.

2 The encyclopedic nature and relative inaccessibility of Habermas's work, however, have produced an enormous number of introductory essays and books intended to acquaint the readership with the basic elements of his thought. McCarthy's critical summary of Habermas's writings is in this regard still the most valuable source, particularly to trace the foundations and intellectual developments of Habermas's earlier work (McCarthy, 1978). For introductions to Habermas's more recent work, see Brand (1990); Holub (1991); Ingram (1987); Rasmussen (1990a); Roderick (1986).

3 The ethics of discourse first elaborated by Habermas (1990a: 43–115) has recently been clarified in relation to its critics (Habermas, 1993). For helpful summary statements of Habermas's moral philosophy, see Ferrara (1985); Heller (1984–5); Rasmussen (1990a: 56–74); Tuori (1989). For discussions on the value and limitations of Habermas's proposals, see the commentaries in Benhabib and Dallmayr (1990); Kelly (1990a); Rasmussen (1990b).

4 The critique that Habermas's ethics of discourse does contain substantive normative propositions, despite its strictly procedural aspirations, has been suggested by Benhabib (1990); Kelly (1990b); Tuori (1989).

5 The indecisively formalistic nature of, and the difficulties in applying, Habermas's moral philosophy are discussed by Döbert (1990); Dwars (1992); Günther (1989; 1990); Heller (1984–5); Pettit (1982). The relevance of this issue for legal studies is well explored in the discussion between Alexy (1992; 1993) and Günther (1993). For a discussion of the human rights perspective in relation to Habermas's legal theory, see Mullen (1986).

6 For introductions to the perspective of Critical Legal Studies, see, for instance, Fitzpatrick and Hunt (1987); Unger (1986). Habermas has occasionally commented upon the Critical Legal Studies approach to law (e.g. Habermas, 1988: 257; 1992a: 261 ff.), and several commentaries have centered on the relationship between Habermas's work and Critical Legal Studies (see Belliotti, 1989; Hoy, 1985; Husson, 1986; Ingram, 1990; and Rasmussen, 1988, 1990a: 75–93).

7 The underlying theme of Habermas's critique is the so-called 'performative contradiction' he argues Critical Legal Studies are subject to. Performative contradiction refers to the fact that the content of an argument contradicts inevitable assumptions of the act of argumentation itself (see Habermas, 1990a: 80–2). Habermas has regularly

employed an analogous mode of critique against deconstructionist and postmodern theories (see Habermas, 1987b), and raised similar arguments against the work of Michel Foucault (Habermas, 1987b: 238–93; 1989a: 173–9; see the discussion in Jay, 1992).

8   The theories of Niklas Luhmann deserve a discussion beyond the scope of this introduction. For an elaboration of Luhmann's legal theory, see Luhmann (1985; 1992). Habermas has criticized Luhmann's project from the standpoint of its systems-theoretical foundations (Habermas, 1987b: 368–85) and its repercussions for the study of law (Habermas, 1988: 251–60). The general contrasts between the theories of Habermas and Luhmann are clarified in Holub (1991: 106–32); and their diverging approaches to law are discussed by Eder (1988); Teubner (1983; 1989).

9   These criticisms of Habermas's approach to law in its original formulation in *The Theory of Communicative Action* are discussed by Raes (1986); van der Burg (1990).

10   Habermas explicated this change in his thoughts on law in several papers published after (the 1981 German original of) *The Theory of Communicative Action* (see, e.g., Habermas, 1988; 1989b; 1990b; 1990c). See also Habermas's discussions on civil disobedience which anticipate the reorientation in his legal theory (see Habermas, 1985; 1992b).

References

Alexy, Robert (1989a) *A Theory of Legal Argumentation*. Oxford: Clarendon Press.

Alexy, Robert (1989b) 'On Necessary Relations Between Law and Morality', *Ratio Juris* 2: 167–83.

Alexy, Robert (1990) 'Problems of Discursive Rationality in Law', in W. Maihofer and G. Sprenger (eds) *Law and the States in Modern Times*. Stuttgart: Franz Steiner.

Alexy, Robert (1992) 'A Discourse-Theoretical Conception of Practical Reason', *Ratio Juris* 5: 231–51.

Alexy, Robert (1993) 'Justification and Application of Norms', *Ratio Juris* 6: 157–70.

Belliotti, Raymond A. (1989) 'Radical Politics and Nonfoundational Morality', *International Philosophical Quarterly* 29: 33.

Benhabib, Seyla (1990) 'In the Shadow of Aristotle and Hegel: Communicative Ethics and Current Controversies in Practical Philosophy', in

M. Kelly (ed.) *Hermeneutics and Critical Theory in Ethics and Politics*. Cambridge, MA: MIT Press.

Benhabib, Seyla and Dallmayr, Fred, eds (1990) *The Communicative Ethics Controversy*. Cambridge, MA: MIT Press.

Brand, Arie (1987) 'Ethical Rationalization and "Juridification": Habermas' Critical Legal Theory', *Australian Journal of Law and Society* 4: 103–27.

Brand, Arie (1990) *The Force of Reason: An Introduction to Habermas' Theory of Communicative Action*. Sydney: Allen & Unwin.

Cole, David (1985) 'Getting There: Reflections on Trashing from Feminist Jurisprudence and Critical Theory', *Harvard Women's Law Journal* 8: 59–91.

Dan-Cohen, Meir (1989) 'Law, Community, and Communication', *Duke Law Journal* 6: 1654–76.

Döbert, Rainer (1990) 'Against the Neglect of Content in the Moral Theories of Kohlberg and Habermas', in T. E. Wren (ed.) *The Moral Domain: Essays in the Ongoing Discussion between Philosophy and the Social Sciences*. Cambridge, MA: MIT Press.

Dwars, Ingrid (1992) 'Application Discourse and the Special Case-Thesis', *Ratio Juris* 5: 67–78.

Eder, Klaus (1988) 'Critique of Habermas' Contribution to the Sociology of Law', *Law and Society Review* 22: 931–44.

Feldman, Stephen M. (1993) 'The Persistence of Power and the Struggle for Dialogic Standards in Postmodern Constitutional Jurisprudence: Michelman, Habermas, and Civic Republicanism', *Georgetown Law Journal* 81: 2243–90.

Felts, Arthur A. and Fields, Charles B. (1988) 'Technical and Symbolic Reasoning: An Application of Habermas' Ideological Analysis to the Legal Arena', *Quarterly Journal of Ideology* 12: 1–15.

Ferrara, Alessandro (1985) 'A Critique of Habermas' Diskursethik', *Telos* 64: 45–74.

Fitzpatrick, Peter and Hunt, Alan (1987) *Critical Legal Studies*. Oxford: Basil Blackwell.

Günther, Klaus (1989) 'A Normative Conception of Coherence for a Discursive Theory of Legal Justification', *Ratio Juris* 2: 155–66.

Günther, Klaus (1990) 'Impartial Application of Moral and Legal Norms: A Contribution to Discourse Ethics', in D. M. Rasmussen (ed.) *Universalism vs. Communitarianism: Contemporary Debates in Ethics*. Cambridge, MA: MIT Press.

Günther, Klaus (1993) 'Critical Remarks on Robert Alexy's "Special-Case Thesis"', *Ratio Juris* 6: 143–56.

Haarscher, Guy (1986) 'Perelman and Habermas', *Law and Philosophy* 5: 331–42.

Habermas, Jürgen (1984) *The Theory of Communicative Action*, Volume

1, *Reason and the Rationalization of Society*. Boston, MA: Beacon Press.

Habermas, Jürgen (1985) 'Civil Disobedience: Litmus Test for the Democratic Constitutional State', *Berkeley Journal of Sociology* 30: 96–116.

Habermas, Jürgen (1987a) *The Theory of Communicative Action*, Volume 2, *System and Lifeworld: A Critique of Functionalist Reason*. Boston, MA: Beacon Press.

Habermas, Jürgen (1987b) *The Philosophical Discourse of Modernity: Twelve Lectures*. Cambridge: Polity Press.

Habermas, Jürgen (1988) 'Law and Morality', in S. M. McMurrin (ed.) *The Tanner Lectures on Human Values*, Volume 8. Salt Lake City: University of Utah Press.

Habermas, Jürgen (1989a) *The New Conservatism: Cultural Criticism and the Historians' Debate*. Cambridge, MA: MIT Press.

Habermas, Jürgen (1989b) 'Towards a Communication-Concept of Rational Collective Will-Formation: A Thought-Experiment', *Ratio Juris* 2: 144–54.

Habermas, Jürgen (1990a) *Moral Consciousness and Communicative Action*. Cambridge, MA: MIT Press.

Habermas, Jürgen (1990b) 'Remarks on the Discussion', *Theory, Culture and Society* 7: 127–32.

Habermas, Jürgen (1990c) 'Morality, Society and Ethics: An Interview with Torben Hviid Nielsen', *Acta Sociologica* 33: 93–114.

Habermas, Jürgen (1992a) *Faktizität und Geltung*. Frankfurt: Suhrkamp.

Habermas, Jürgen (1992b) 'On Morality, Law, Civil Disobedience and Modernity', in P. Dews (ed.) *Autonomy and Solidarity: Interviews with Jürgen Habermas*, revised edn. London: Verso.

Habermas, Jürgen (1993) *Justification and Application: Remarks on Discourse Ethics*. Cambridge, MA: MIT Press.

Habermas, Jürgen (1994) 'Nachwort (zur vierten, durchgesehenen und um ein Literaturverzeichnis ergänzten Auflage)', in J. Habermas, *Faktizität und Geltung*, 4th edn. Frankfurt: Suhrkamp.

Habermas, Jürgen (forthcoming) *Between Facts and Norms*. Cambridge, MA: MIT Press.

Heller, Agnes (1984–5) 'The Discourse Ethics of Habermas: Critique and Appraisal', *Thesis Eleven* 10/11: 5–17.

Holub, Robert C. (1991) *Jürgen Habermas: Critic in the Public Sphere*. London: Routledge.

Hoy, David C. (1985) 'Interpreting the Law: Hermeneutical and Post-structuralist Perspectives', *Southern California Law Review* 58: 135–76.

Husson, Christine A. Desan (1986) 'Expanding the Legal Vocabulary:

The Challenge Posed by the Deconstruction and Defense of Law', *Yale Law Journal* 95: 969–91.

Ingram, David (1987) *Habermas and the Dialectic of Reason*. New Haven, CT: Yale University Press.

Ingram, David (1990) 'Dworkin, Habermas, and the CLS Movement on Moral Criticism in Law', *Philosophy and Social Criticism* 16: 237–68.

Jay, Martin (1992) 'The Debate over Performative Contradiction', in A. Honneth, T. McCarthy, C. Offe and A. Wellmer (eds) *Philosophical Interventions in the Unfinished Project of Enlightenment*. Cambridge, MA: MIT Press.

Kelly, Michael, ed. (1990a) *Hermeneutics and Critical Theory in Ethics and Politics*. Cambridge, MA: MIT Press.

Kelly, Michael (1990b), 'MacIntyre, Habermas and Philosophical Ethics', in M. Kelly (ed.) *Hermeneutics and Critical Theory in Ethics and Politics*. Cambridge, MA: MIT Press.

Leedes, Gary C. (1991) 'The Discourse Ethics Alternative to Rust v. Sullivan', *University of Richmond Law Review* 26: 87–143.

Luhmann, Niklas (1985) *A Sociological Theory of Law*. London: Routledge & Kegan Paul.

Luhmann, Niklas (1992) 'Operational Closure and Structural Coupling: The Differentiation of the Legal System', *Cardozo Law Review* 13: 1419–41.

McCarthy, Thomas (1978) *The Critical Theory of Jürgen Habermas*. Cambridge, MA: MIT Press.

Mootz, Francis J. (1988) 'The Ontological Basis of Legal Hermeneutics: A Proposed Model of Inquiry Based on the Work of Gadamer, Habermas, and Ricoeur', *Boston University Law Review* 68: 523–617.

Mullen, T. (1986) 'Constitutional Protection of Human Rights', in T. Campbell, D. Goldberg, S. McLean and T. Mullen (eds) *Human Rights: From Rhetoric to Reality*. Oxford: Basil Blackwell.

Murphy, W. T. (1989) 'The Habermas Effect: Critical Theory and Academic Law', *Current Legal Problems* 42: 135–65.

Northey, Rod (1988) 'Conflicting Principles of Canadian Environmental Reform: Trubek and Habermas v. Law and Economics and the Law Reform Commission', *Dalhousie Law Journal* 11: 639–62.

Pettit, Philip (1982) 'Habermas on Truth and Justice', in G. H. R. Parkinson (ed.) *Marx and Marxisms*. Cambridge: Cambridge University Press.

Preuss, Ulrich K. (1989) 'Rationality Potentials of Law: Allocative, Distributive and Communicative Rationality', in C. Joerges and D. M. Trubek (eds) *Critical Legal Thought: An American-German Debate*. Baden-Baden: Nomos.

Raes, Koen (1986) 'Legalisation, Communication and Strategy: A Critique of Habermas' Approach to Law', *Journal of Law and Society* 13: 183–206.

Rasmussen, David M. (1988) 'Communication Theory and the Critique of the Law: Habermas and Unger on the Law', *Praxis International* 8: 155–70.

Rasmussen, David M. (1990a) *Reading Habermas*. Oxford: Basil Blackwell.

Rasmussen, David M., ed. (1990b) *Universalism vs. Communitarianism: Contemporary Debates in Ethics*. Cambridge, MA: MIT Press.

Roderick, Rick (1986) *Habermas and the Foundations of Critical Theory*. London: Macmillan.

Scheuerman, Bill (1993) 'Neumann v. Habermas: The Frankfurt School and the Case of the Rule of Law', *Praxis International* 13: 50–67.

Solum, Lawrence B. (1989) 'Freedom of Communicative Action: A Theory of the First Amendment Freedom of Speech', *Northwestern University Law Review* 83: 54–135.

Teubner, Günther (1983) 'Substantive and Reflexive Elements in Modern Law', *Law and Society Review* 17: 239–85.

Teubner, Günther (1989) 'How the Law Thinks: Toward a Constructivist Epistemology of Law', *Law and Society Review* 23: 727–57.

Tuori, Kaarlo (1989) 'Discourse Ethics and the Legitimacy of Law', *Ratio Juris* 2: 125–43.

Unger, Robert M. (1986) *The Critical Legal Studies Movement*. Cambridge, MA: Harvard University Press.

van der Burg, Wibren (1990) 'Jürgen Habermas on Law and Morality: Some Critical Comments', *Theory, Culture and Society* 7: 105–11.

David M. Rasmussen

How is valid law possible?

A review of *Between Facts and Norms* by Jürgen Habermas

German culture has produced two great theoretical discourses on law represented in the work of Hegel and Weber respectively; now, with the publication of Habermas's *Faktizität und Geltung*, it may lay claim to a third. While Hegel found a concrete demonstration of his reflexive philosophy of intersubjective recognition in law, Weber found the study of law to be the key to social integration through legal domination. Habermas has not only learned from but triumphed over both. From Hegel he learned the absolutely central role that law plays in a social philosophy not only as demonstrative of the achievements of a certain form of rationality but also as the representation of the way in which forms of rationality can be demonstrated to exist in a public and institutional realm. From Weber he learned that, in the absence of other forms of social integration, law in modern society performs the sociological role of legitimating through domination. However, contrary to Hegel, Habermas has tied the development of law neither to the political economy of production nor to the rational independence of the state. And, contrary to Weber, although law represents a form of necessary coercion for Habermas, it can be discursively, which is to say normatively, redeemed. Neither Hegel nor Weber, it could be said in retrospect, really understood the explosive force that democracy had and continues to have in shaping modern legal institutions; Habermas does. In fact, the democratic thrust of Habermas's philosophy of law gives it its distinctive character.

How is valid law possible?

I Between facticity and validity

If one were to reconstruct the basis from which this enormously rich and complex book originates, it might be from a question which at least on the surface appears to be deceptively simple: how is valid law possible? Or to put the question another way, what grants validity to law? Of course, the seeming simplicity of the question is apparent only because an answer requires that one must approach the complex and controversial issues associated with the nature of law, its proper domain, its structure and function, within a larger sociopolitical and institutional context. Beyond that an answer requires a hard philosophical justification not only of the term 'validity' but also of validity as it pertains to law.

The problem is where to begin. The book starts with a straightforward presentation and defense of the claims of communicative reason. It could have begun elsewhere. Those familiar with Habermas's earlier work should be familiar with the previous claims of communicative reason. What is unique to this presentation is the attempt to place the claims of communicative reason in the context of a proposed tension between facticity and validity. The argument, which is one constructed against the various claims of both practical reason and post-Nietzschian critique of reason, attempts to ground the split between facticity and validity in the 20th-century claims of linguistic philosophy. Briefly, while practical reason is said to be limited by its inability to free itself from its bondage to context or in this case facticity (the post-Nietzschian critique of reason can be successful only at the expense of reason itself from which it claims to be free) the turn to language philosophy means that the claims of rationality can be discovered as 'inscribed in the linguistic telos of reaching an understanding'. As is well known to those familiar with Habermas's earlier work, the linguistic taking-over of the process of reaching an understanding redeems philosophy from its commitments to a philosophy of the subject, while at the same time enabling philosophers to give an intersubjective account of rational action without getting mired in the 19th-century problems of subjectivity. The assumption here is that the conditions involved in the process of reaching an understanding are the ones which require those addressed to take a performative attitude involving a commitment to certain presuppositions. This means that participants who are involved in the process of reaching an understanding 'must' pursue their goals, goals which may be defined as 'illocutionary', without reservation. Quite simply, ideally conceived, participants in the process of reaching an understanding would be obligated to act according to the agreements reached as a result of that process. But this would be true if and only if the claims implicit in the agreements were valid. Hence, one could argue, as does Habermas, that validity would be at the heart of the process of reaching an understanding.

Given these basic assumptions about reaching an understanding it is Habermas's assumption that validity is attainable only through processes of idealization, an idealization which is juxtaposed to the ordinary course of empirical understanding. In other words, in order to reach an agreement about the validity of a certain claim put forth in the process of reaching an understanding it is necessary to juxtapose facticity and validity. In this view, individuals who act communicatively must involve themselves in certain 'idealizations' concerning commitment to 'pragmatic presuppositions of a contrafactual sort'. On the basis of these kinds of assumptions regarding the process of reaching an understanding and the rationality implicit in that process Habermas posits the following thesis: 'A set of unavoidable idealizations forms the counterfactual basis of a factual practice of reaching an understanding that is directed critically against its own results and can *transcend* itself.'[1] Habermas further believes that it follows from this thesis that the 'tension between idea and reality breaks into the very facticity of linguistically structured forms of everyday life'.[2]

A brief look at the contributions of 20th-century language philosophy could help clarify the relationship of facticity and validity. While Frege's unique contribution was to understand that thoughts are discovered through representations, meaning that thoughts are equal to states of affairs represented in sentences, the peculiar form of idealization that emerged from that line of investigation resulted in a form of typification that could only refer to the internal structure of language. In that context, reference was conceived as 'grammatical invariance' associated with the general structure of language. The breakthrough, again from this point of view, was the discovery of the assertorial sentence which managed to move out of the internal framework of semantic reference. Habermas's claim is that with an assertion a 'speaker raises a criticizable claim to the validity of the asserted sentence; and because no one has direct access to uninterpreted conditions of validity, "validity" must be understood epistemically as "validity proven for us"'.[3] In the former view, the semantic view, idealization refers to the underlying discovery of the 'rule structure of language' which transcends and informs ordinary linguistic usage. In the latter view, the pragmatic view, idealization affects validity because validity is both implicit in and transcends agreement.

Habermas assumes that this tension between facticity and validity which inhabits the very heart of language affects the social order as well. This assumption is predicated on the belief that the insights derived from speech-act theory are embedded in the presuppositions of everyday communicative practice. If this is true then the idealizations which are implicit in language, the illocutionary binding/bonding forces of speech-acts, are 'enlisted for the coordination of the action plans of different actors'.[4] In a sense the thesis Habermas is building at this point, which is essential for the argumentative structure of the book, is that what is true for language, so interpreted, is true for society as well. And if one can claim that this is the case, then it is possible to pose a further question: from the point of view of society, what stabilizes the relationship between facticity and validity? The premiss of the thesis may be stated in the following way: 'With the concept of communicative action, which brings in mutual linguistic understanding as a mechanism of action coordination, the counterfactual suppositions of actors who orient their action to validity claims also acquire immediate relevance for the construction and preservation of the social order: for this order *subsists* through the recognition of normative validity claims.'[5] This would mean that the fundamental claims about a rationality, which has as its focus the process of reaching an understanding, would contain assumptions not only about the nature of language but about society as well. As Habermas puts it: 'This means that the tension between facticity and validity built into language and its use returns in the dynamics of the integration of socialized, or at least communicatively socialized, individuals – and must be worked off by the participants' own efforts.'[6] Here, we are but one step away from the about-to-unfold drama of the special way in which the tension between facticity and validity is stabilized in society. In that drama, as we shall see, law will play the central role.

To this linguistically mediated argument regarding the tension between facticity and validity, Habermas offers a second based on something of a thought experiment. From the point of view of the stability of the social order, archaic institutions could be conceived as institutions which represent a fusion of facticity and validity, a link which is sustained and reinforced later by sacred authority. However, when society becomes more complex and social differentiation occurs through secularization allowing actors to make a distinction between communicative and strategic interaction, law emerges as a mode of integration stabilizing the separation between facticity and validity. According to Habermas this allows us to explain modern forms of social integration. Whereas archaic institutions represented a fusion of facticity and validity, and later institutions required a conception of authority to hold the link between facticity and validity in place, in modernity mutual understanding replaces authority as the mechanism for mediating the spheres formerly regulated by habit and custom. But this is not an easy problem because with secularization the strong institutions which were the guarantors of social integration have been undermined allowing a certain social dissension to grow. The dilemma revolves around the problem of how can the 'differentiated lifeworlds that are internally pluralized and disenchanted be socially integrated'? In discourse-theoretic terms, the strategic and the communicative have become separated. Habermas speculates that the 'only way out of this predicament is for the actors themselves *to reach an understanding* about the *normative regulation of strategic interactions*'.[7] In other words, the classical problem in modern political philosophy emerges. Norms must be imposed and responded to in order to guarantee the mere cohesion and stability of the social order, while at the same time appearing to be rational. The problem is simply one of keeping the social order intact while at the same time appealing to its implicit rational foundations. In discourse-theoretic terms, how can the realms of communicative and strategic action which have become separated and which are perceived to be incompatible, be integrated without dissolving one into the other? The answer will be conceived in terms of law. Hence, we return to the question from which we began, namely, what counts for validity in law?

One might note that although the question has not been answered, it has been framed in discourse-theoretic terms. In terms of the classic discussions of political philosophy, when Hobbes attempts to get his readers to agree to the proposition that the only way out of the war of all against all is through consent, explicitly to the rule of a sovereign and implicitly to the terms of a compact made with one's political consociates, indirectly the question of the validity of law is assumed. In Kant and Rousseau the question is posed even more radically because they take seriously the necessity for compliance with the law and its claims to legitimacy. In discourse-theoretic terms the tension between facticity and validity manifests itself because 'enacted law cannot secure the basis of its legitimacy simply through legality, which leaves attitudes and motives up to the addressees'.[8] Or in the terms that Rousseau and Kant framed the issue, 'the claim to legitimacy on the part of a legal order built on rights can only be redeemed through the socially integrative force of the "concurring and united will of all free and equal citizens"'. The discourse-theoretic reading of the place of law seeks to take up the classical problematic, but not by the route of philosophy alone.

II Between philosophy and sociology

There are essentially two things a philosophy and/or sociology of law must do: it must show how law interfaces with standards of normativity while at the same time not collapsing law into morality and it must show how law must be the linchpin in a theory of social integration while at the same time not identifying law too closely with a strategy of social domination. The former issue is defined classically as the association between law and justice while the latter is associated with sociological explanation in the wake of secularization. Philosophers from Plato on have erred by making law conform totally to the standards of morality, while sociologists like Weber make an effective case for a theory of social integration through law which accounted for the emergence of secular authority but at the price of subsuming the emergence of law to the category of power. The problem cannot be one which finds law to be the servant of either power or justice. Obviously, it must be conceived in the context of both. From the sociological perspective, law must be authoritative enough to force social integration after the great religious traditions have lost their normative authority. From the philosophical perspective law must have some kind of basis in justice which will enable, particularly in a burgeoning democratic society, willful assent to its legitimacy.

In this attempt to mediate between philosophy and sociology Habermas finds Rawls and Luhmann wanting, while in the tradition of Weber, Parsons and Durkheim, Habermas builds a theoretical framework from which the validity dimension of law can be reconstructed. The point against Rawls, which will be debated, is that Rawls attempts to legitimate his concept of justice through just institutions particularly as his theory of justice has developed. If this is true then just institutions, rather than – to anticipate later arguments – the procedural mechanism for social integration, will bear the brunt of grounding valid law. This 'thin theory of the good' would anchor 'individual morality' in 'just institutions' because it assumes along with Hegel that such institutions 'would create circumstances under which it would lie in each one's well-considered interest to pursue one's own freely chosen life plans under the same conditions that are granted to other persons so they can pursue their life plans'.[9] Of course, having so characterized Rawls the next step in the argument can be anticipated. Echoing Plato's classical argument regarding justice, arguments based on just institutions are valid only if just institutions exist. Here, the sociological side of the argument can be used against Rawls. Rawls finds the stabilizing force of social institutions to be derived from just institutions rather than from the coercive force of the law and the mechanism which integrates that coercive force. Rawls does not develop a philosophy of law, argues Habermas, but if he did he would have to return to the problems of the normative reconstruction, which he faced in his earlier period, for the conditions of valid law independent of a theory of just institutions. One can only do that by reconstructing the normative foundation of legal validity from a social-scientific point of view. This is a key part of the argument because it shows the manner in which this dual philosophical-sociological approach can be used to critique the underlying assumptions of a purely philosophical approach.

This brief discussion of Rawls is central because it illustrates what Habermas thinks he can do by combining the normative with the sociological approach to the problem of validity in law. However, the move from philosophy to sociology does not automatically guarantee a more comprehensive approach. In fact, Luhmann's system-theoretic approach is rejected on grounds opposite to those of Rawls. One can anticipate the argument. If Rawls is rejected because he attempts to ground justice on just institutions, Luhmann is rejected because he eliminates the question of normativity altogether. By conceiving of law as an autonomous system Luhmann is said to 'obliterate' all 'traces' of 'normative self-understanding of the legal system in classical social theory'. Hence, Luhmann is characterized as one who can derive the 'validity' of law only 'positivistically', 'from existing law'.

For Habermas this dual critique sets up the argument for a social-scientific discourse on law which will consider not only its normative but also its institutional dimension. Here, the argument takes its point of departure from the classical Weberian thesis regarding secularization. Secularization will be said to involve a rationalization process that while undermining the 'metasocial guarantees of the legal order' does not 'vaporize ... the non-instrumentalizable quality of the law's claim to legitimacy'.[10] This would mean that the normative foundation on which law's claim to legitimacy rests would be transferred from a sacred to a secular authority. Weber believed this force to be that of 'political domination'. Habermas maintains that Weber failed to understand the 'specific socially integrative function of law' because he assumed that the 'constitutional state' does not depend upon 'the democratic form of political will-formation', but rather is derived from 'political domination'. In this view, if one takes Weber's perspective seriously, the result is a specifically 'German' interpretation of 'modern government by law', a view which accommodates the 'elitist domination of political parties'. Hence, in this view, and this is certainly one of the major insights contained in the book, Weber is right about secularization but wrong about rationalization. Certainly, Habermas has made this point elsewhere, but not with the same originality as here. If the socially integrative force is not political domination, what is it? Habermas uses Parsons's concept of the 'juridification of political power' and Durkheim's concept of the 'evolution of the societal community' in relationship to law to restate the Weberian thesis on secularization. In its most elementary form the thesis replaces 'political domination' with 'democratic will-formation'. Durkheim's concept of 'societal community' becomes in modern terms, 'civil society'. Hence, the wager: 'modern law can stabilize behavior expectations in a complex society with structurally differentiated lifeworlds and functionally independent subsystems only if law, as regent for a "societal community" that has transformed itself into civil society, can maintain the inherited claim to solidarity in the abstract form of a believable claim to legitimacy'.[11] It is precisely this democratic reading which will inform Habermas's reconstruction of the place of law in modern society. One might also anticipate that it is this view which will characterize this reading of modern law as distinctive.

III Reconstructing law: rights and the constitutional state

1 Rights

Having made the case for the tension between facticity and validity and having shown that law must somehow mediate between philosophical claims for justification and sociological accounts of institutionalization, Habermas is now in a position to 'rationally reconstruct the *self-understanding* of . . . modern legal orders'. It is at this level that one can begin to answer the question from which our inquiry began, namely, how is valid law possible? Thus far, the argument has established that law must meet the following conditions: not only must it provide the basis for the 'social integration of economic societies', but also it must 'satisfy the precarious conditions of a social integration that ultimately takes place through the achievements of mutual understanding on the part of communicatively acting subjects, i.e. through the acceptability of validity claims'.[12] Put simply, law holds society together through the power of enforcement. Law is a coercive instrument. But the condition for the possibility of its coercive implementation is that it is valid. In order for law to be valid it must derive its legitimacy from those to whom it is applied. If one begins with rights, as the modern political-philosophical tradition did, then the problem becomes one of determining 'the rights citizens must accord one another if they want to legitimately regulate their living together by means of positive law'.[13] As the political tradition saw, rights which are 'subjective liberties' must be observed as obligations. However, in order to be legitimate they must be derived from 'democratic legislative procedures' which 'confront its participants with the normative expectations of the orientation to the common good'. This would mean that there must be a fundamental connection between human rights and popular sovereignty. In Kant this relationship was sought in the derivation of individual autonomy from the universal law, while in Rousseau, who came closer to the truth, it was found in the attempt to correlate the individual and the general will. This is where the democratic reading of the formation of modern law pays off. 'The sought-for internal connection between popular sovereignty and human rights lies in the normative content of a mode of exercising political autonomy, a mode that is not secured simply through the form of general laws but only through the communicative form of discursive processes of opinion and will-formation.'[14] Habermas seeks to take the argument a step beyond the overly subjective character of the tradition by applying the insights of speech-act theory to the dilemma of deriving public rights from subjective liberties. The assumption is that private and public autonomy are 'co-original'. This, it is argued, can be comprehended when it is understood that the 'substance of human rights . . . resides in the formal conditions for the legal institutionalization of those discursive processes of opinion – and will-formation in which the sovereignty of a people assumes a practical shape'.[15] In other words, the assumptions of mutual respect and equal application are written into the very discursive shape of the process of reaching an understanding which derives autonomy intersubjectively.

Here, we can begin to consider the question of valid law in a more concrete fashion. From the point of view of a system of rights, rights 'should not only institutionalize a rational political will-formation, but should also guarantee the very medium in which this will-formation can express itself as a common will of freely associated consociates under law'.[16] Law is indeed regulative in the sense that it harbors certain expectations assuming that one has the 'capacity' for 'purposive-rational decisions, i.e., the capacity for freedom of choice'. From a sociological perspective the emergence of the legal form occurs with the 'collapse of traditional ethical life'. Hence, that which gives validity to law at this point in the discussion is the assumption that in the pragmatic application and derivation of a legal norm, not only need law be enforceable but it must appeal to the assent of the governed, if only hypothetically. Legal norms would ideally be traceable to legislative decisions and juridical reformulations which would require such conceptualization. Without going into the very difficult and, to be sure, controversial issue of the relationship between morality and law, or moral norms and legal norms, Habermas's strategy with regard to rights has been, by giving 'equal weight' to private and public autonomy, to avoid the traditional problem of trying to deduce public from private autonomy. For this conception of the derivation of right, Habermas adopts Klaus Günther's term 'communicative freedom' which refers to the 'possibility participants engaged in the effort to reach an understanding mutually presuppose, i.e. the possibility of adopting a position to the utterances of one's counterpart and to the concomitantly raised validity claims, which depend on intersubjective recognition'.[17]

2 The constitutional state

The second part of the reconstructive argument deals directly with the question of law and power. The state is the mechanism for rendering 'permanent' the system of rights as well as the enforcement of the law. The state accounts for the other, strategic side of the argument. But the problem of the state is a tricky one. If one defines the relationship of the state in alliance with political power too closely, one will lose the independent claim to validity which has been established in the prior discourse on rights. In German thought Hegel provided the example by associating the state with rational necessity. Hence, although the state 'becomes necessary as a sanctioning, organizing and executive power', Habermas argues, 'at the post-traditional level of justification only those laws count as legitimate that could be accepted by all legal consociates in a discursive process of opinion- and will-formation'.[18]

In order to conceive the place of law within the state Habermas attempts an imaginary reconstruction of the origin and development of the state in terms of a two-stage model. Ideally, or contrafactually, conceived, in the first stage a 'royal judge' would 'monopolize the function of conflict resolution' while in the second stage the 'legal institutionalization of a ruling staff that makes collective will-formation possible' would make possible an 'organized form of political domination'.[19] In the first stage the leader who has social power and administers through sacred power, combines two functions, the authorization of power by sacred law and the sanctioning of social power by sacred power. In the second stage, law is a means of social integration while at the same time one of legitimating political power. Thus, the state is allowed to make legally binding decisions which simultaneously organize society.

The model would then solve the riddle of the origin of political domination. 'As soon as law bestows a legal form on political domination it serves the constitution of a binary power code. Whoever disposes over power can give commands to others.'[20] Law would play a key role in this process because it would serve as 'the means of organizing state authority'.[21] It would appear, again following Habermas, that from this model one can see not only that political power engenders a 'certainty of law' but also that codification would arise which would provide the rules of law with a certain 'consistency'. From this task would arise jurisprudence. However, it would appear that if political power grants 'certainty' to law and if jurisprudence grants 'consistency' to law, it would still be the case that law would have to appeal to justice for its legitimacy. And finally, if we look at this contrafactual model from the point of view of historical development, it would appear that forms of legitimation change. If it is the case originally that legal domination occurs largely through state power, it would appear that eventually law must be legitimated through processes of justification.

Again, speculating on the basis of the contrafactual model, there are reasons for this. One could assume that originally law had a sacred foundation. However, with the passage to modernity sacred law lost its 'metaphysical dignity and indisponibility'. The result was that 'a legitimation gap opened up in the cyclic exchange between instrumentally conceived power and instrumentalized law'.[22] And if this were the case, Habermas could make the substantial claim that 'reason' would replace the 'sacred resources of justice'. From this hypothetical argument Habermas can make his claim against Weber. The issue revolves around the designation of the particular kind of reason that it is. For Weber that form of reason was associated with purposive-rational action. Habermas here makes his claim for communicative reason based on speech-act theory. The opening of this legitimation gap left room for the emergence of a certain kind of 'communicative power' which has its source in the formation of opinion. This would mean that in the Weberian model one could only conceive of the emergence of reason instrumentally or strategically, while in this model the emergence of communicative power would allow one to elaborate reason by analogy to speech-act theory, i.e. communicatively. Hence, Habermas claims that what opened up was a kind of productive reason which could create a 'new social fact'. This is associated with the 'intersubjective recognition' of 'validity claims' raised in 'speech-acts' reinforcing 'a belief held in common' which is held by a 'speaker and the hearer' involving 'tacit acceptance of obligations relevant for action'. This reading will contrast radically with the pure strategic reading of the claims of the modern state sustained by Weber. And, it will allow one to read the development of the modern state from the perspective of the '*close kinship of communicative action with the production of legitimate law*'.[23] Also, it will allow Habermas to argue that law can be viewed as the 'medium through which communicative power is translated into administrative power'.[24]

IV Jurisprudence and rationality

Habermas, having worked out a theory of rationality in relationship to the validity of law, can now turn to argue his case against the formidable opponents in the field of the philosophy of law or jurisprudence. It is of some note that his chapter entitled 'The Indeterminacy of the Law and the Rationality of Adjudication', assumes that the fundamental issue in adjudication is the 'rationality problem'. Importantly, at this point in the argument he is able to approach jurisprudence from the perspective of rationality because he has not only developed the idea of communicative rationality but also, in contrast to Weber's account, he has constructed an alternative and much more positive account of the relationship of reason to law. Echoing Hegel, Habermas defines the 'rationality problem' in the form of a question: 'How can the application of a contingently emergent law be carried out with internal consistency and grounded in an externally rational way so as to guarantee simultaneously the *certainty of law* and its *rightness*?'[25] The problem arises in the absence of natural law which could give assurances regarding both certainty and rightness. According to this view legal decisions have to be both 'consistent' and 'rationally acceptable'. Hence, adjudication is said to reach beyond the decision by the courts through the imposition of standards which can claim a wider reference.

The strategy of this chapter is to locate the various contemporary philosophical approaches to law, legal hermeneutics, legal realism, legal positivism and, to some extent, Critical Legal Studies, in the context of the rationality problem. Regardless of whether or not this strategy works, it is designed to bring us to a particular view of the way in which philosophical-sociological theory should inform legal interpretation. Equally, it assumes a certain dissociation for purposes of theoretical presentation between issues of facticity and those of validity. One finds that each position analyzed will be unable to address the rationality problem because it will have failed to make the appropriate distinction between facticity and validity which in turn will expose a vulnerability on the question of validity.

The critique of legal hermeneutics, which is the most venerable of the positions examined in the sense that it alone predates modernity, is based on the very embeddedness of interpretation. In essence the claim is that the standards for interpretation are relative because they are only referable to the *preunderstanding* of the judge. In turn the preunderstanding of the judge is shaped by the 'ethical complex of tradition'. Legal hermeneutics is then characterized as an essentially contextualist position which, because of its very location within tradition, cannot reach out for standards beyond tradition. It is claimed that the principles used in processes of adjudication can only be 'legitimated from the effective history of those forms of law and life in which judges continually find themselves'.[26] No doubt this critique reflects the deep suspicion held by Habermas regarding so-called contextualist positions in both law and moral theory. In this view context-dependent positions are bound by traditions which may be oppressive. The overcoming of such context-dependent positions requires forms of idealization which, as we have seen, separate facticity from validity. As we shall see in a moment, hermeneutics, in accord with this argument, when elevated to the status of critical hermeneutics, bears a trace of idealization which upon examination leads to a discourse theory of law. Further, it is the hermeneutic position which is the most noble because, although its standards are context dependent, it does at least have standards which have a moral reference, even though it may be said to err because the position makes no real distinction between ethics and morality, a distinction which is fundamental to discourse theory.

Legal realism and legal positivism do not play as well in this critique. Legal realism is said to be a kind of skepticism while legal positivism is dismissed under the rules of the classic critique of positivism; essentially it cannot justify its own principles. 'The legitimation of the legal order shifts to its origin, i.e. to a Basic Norm or rule of recognition that legitimates everything without itself being capable of rational justification: as part of a historical form of life it must be accepted de facto as settled custom, i.e. as a kind of habit.'[27] The critique of legal realism is carried on in the shadow of Critical Legal Studies which has attempted to show that there is essentially no difference between judicial decisions and political policy decisions. The claim is that legal realists are basically skeptics who attribute judicial decision-making to a host of factors, interests, class, political alignments, power, etc. And if they are skeptics they cannot meet the standards of the rationality problem. 'The realists cannot explain how the functional capacity of the legal system is compatible with a radical legal skepticism on the part of involved experts.'[28] In the end the claim is that neither legal realism nor legal positivism can resolve the rationality problem as it has been put forth by Habermas.

The most interesting, and one might add controversial, aspect of this strategy of critique is to be found in the role that the interpretation of Ronald Dworkin's legal philosophy plays. The central thesis is that Dworkin is said to have constructed a 'critical hermeneutics' which in contrast to ordinary legal hermeneutics is not associated with the 'preunderstanding of normative transmissions' but rather with the 'critical appropriation of the institutional history of law'. According to this interpretation, Dworkin takes legal philosophy beyond context-dependent, historical reference by incorporating a moment of idealization into the analysis. As such he overcomes the limitations of legal hermeneutics, legal realism and legal positivism which in various ways were said to be context dependent. Habermas reads Dworkin as having contributed essentially two dimensions which are said to be absent in the prior positions; first, that legal decisions may have reference to a certain moral content and, second, that moral content goes beyond a particular historical context. Dworkin simply does this, it is claimed, by appealing to principle. For example, precisely because legal positivism did not appeal to principles outside the legal system in situations of conflict (hard cases) it had to resort to the possibly arbitrary decisions of judges to make its case. Hence, it had to resolve 'indeterminacy' in a 'decisionistic' manner. The appeal to principle will get us beyond the assumption that law is a 'closed . . . rule system' which in the case of conflict results in a certain 'indeterminacy'. It is important to note that Habermas interprets the appeal to principle as 'higher-level justification of norm applications'.[29] And it is precisely this appeal to principle which is said to differentiate Dworkin from normal hermeneutics. 'Since these principles cannot in turn be drawn like historically proven topoi from an ethical community's complex of received traditions, as legal hermeneutics assumes, the practice of interpretation requires a point of reference that takes one beyond settled legal traditions.'[30] This is the controversial point. Dworkin's appeal to principle is rather easily woven into the Habermasian narrative about the necessity for justification. Critical hermeneutics is said to appeal to a certain form of ahistoricality which in turn will lead to the separation of context-dependent historical evidence from theory. According to this interpretation, 'Dworkin explains this reference point of practical reason methodologically in terms of the procedure of constructive interpretation. He explains it substantively by postulating a legal theory that rationally reconstructs and articulates valid law at a given time.'[31] So Dworkin, like Habermas, is interpreted to go through procedures of 'rational reconstruction' which will justify and account procedurally for the phenomenon of validity in law. Whether Dworkin would go along with this characterization of his own theory is, of course, open to question. In order to develop this approach to Dworkin's thought it is necessary to interpret the Dworkin of *Law's Empire* through *Taking Rights Seriously* and *A Matter of Principle*. For example, when Dworkin says in *Law's Empire* 'Constructive interpretation is a matter of imposing purpose on an object or practice in order to make of it the best possible example of the form or genre to which it is taken to belong',[32] it is interpreted to mean the following: 'With the help of such a procedure of constructive interpretation each judge should be able in principle to reach an ideally valid decision by supporting his justification on a "theory", thereby compensating for the supposed "indeterminacy of law".'[33]

If one follows Habermas's line of interpretation, the claim of principle on Dworkin's part leads to the larger defense of a doctrine of coherence which Dworkin the hermeneuticist puts in the hands of the judge. Hercules is able to overcome the doctrine of indeterminacy in the law because he is able to appeal to the 'best theory possible' and conduct 'rational reconstruction'. Equally, by upholding the classical principle of 'integrity' Hercules is able to sustain the interpretation of the law on the basis of ideals derived from the political community. 'The judge's obligation to decide the individual case in the light of a theory justifying valid law as a whole on the basis of principles reflects a prior obligation of citizens, attested by the act of founding the constitution, to maintain the integrity of their life in common by following principles of justice and respecting each other as members of an association of free and equal persons.'[34]

Habermas's contention is that although Dworkin is on the right track, Dworkin's hero is unable to carry the program out because the 'integrity' of the judge is not enough. One would have to liberate Hercules from the 'loneliness of a monologically conducted theory construction'. Frank Michelman referred to Hercules as a 'loner'. Habermas will elaborate this point by bringing his detailed critique of subjectivity to bear on the point. Dworkin has acknowledged that integrity is somehow grounded in equal right. If one acknowledges equal right to subjective liberties, the question is, should these equal rights be anchored in the 'ideal personality of a judge who distinguishes himself by his virtue and his privileged access to the truth'? Wouldn't it be better to ground the 'ideal demands of legal theory' in another ideal, namely, the 'ideal of an open society of interpreters of the constitution'? In this view, a theory of interpretation would necessarily refer beyond the immediacy of a judgment of an individual to the intersubjectivity of a community of interpreters conceived along the lines of a discourse theory of law, the theoretical foundations of which we have already witnessed in the first chapter of Habermas's book.

How is valid law possible?

V Judiciary and legislation

If it is the case that the modern constitutional state has been established through the process of democratic will-formation which can be reconstructed along the lines of private and public autonomy which ideally conceived would follow the principles of a form of rationality as set forth in a discourse theory of law, would not the role of judges and the judiciary be significantly altered? Further, if the role of the judiciary were to be altered would it not also transform the role of supreme courts who assert the right of judicial review? As in Habermas's prior chapter, where individual judgment is critiqued in the name of the so-called community of interpreters of the constitution, so, in the one entitled 'The Judiciary and Legislation: On the Role and Legitimacy of Constitutional Adjudication', which attempts to take a look at supreme courts where the competition over legitimacy between the legislature and the courts becomes intense, Habermas must give to the supreme courts as he did to judges a role, without at the same time sacrificing his account of public rationality. Here, Habermas hits a classic problem, namely, how to make the institutions of the day fit with an ideally conceived theory of rationality. There is an underlying issue which the theory would like to account for, namely, that of making both judges and courts ever more accountable to democratic constituencies. In Anglo-Saxon jurisprudence, judges have been belligerent in their desire to retain their right to make judgments in accord with their own wisdom without having to account for theories of rationality propounded by philosophers. The problem is magnified at the level of supreme courts where the wisdom of the courts and that of the legislative are often in radical conflict. The recent Thomas hearings in the United States which represented the potential of a supreme court to repeal both a prior supreme court opinion and the public will, and the recent repeal by the German Constitutional Court of legislative determinations on abortion represent cases in point. Indeed, they bring into question the matter of validity in a concrete way, i.e. the validity of court procedures in reference not only to law but also to political processes.

Habermas's strategy is to conceive of the issue paradigmatically. The thesis is that the role of the court can be conceived by analogy to the form of the state it is designed to serve. The argument draws on his earlier attempt to conceive private and public autonomy as co-original. There Habermas argued that the failure of the liberal paradigm was to derive rights from private autonomy. Here, under the liberal paradigm the Supreme Court would exist to defend the rights of individuals, rights which have been conceived as represented through legislative decisions that have now become valid law. Under the liberal paradigm the constitution separated the activity of the courts from the politics of the state and economic society. Basic rights were conceived to be rights of the individual against the state. With the growth of the welfare state this model began to lose its force not only because of the growth of the power of the state as against the autonomy of the individual, but also because of the expansion of the domain of constitutional law into the realm of political power. There are arguments which would attempt to retrieve the liberal paradigm in the new, welfare-state, context. But, as we have seen, in Habermas's view, the liberal procedural paradigm is itself flawed. As a result Habermas wants to ally himself with those who would rethink the model of supreme court adjudication along the lines which would lead to a deliberative paradigm as opposed to either a liberal or welfare-state paradigm.

The task becomes one of reconceptualizing the role of the court under the deliberative paradigm. In order to do this, Habermas enters a German debate over the 'doctrine of values' developed in reference to the German Constitutional Court. The claim is that the Constitutional Court understands law not as a 'system of rules structured by principles' but as a 'concrete value order'. The hidden premise underlying such a view of the court is that the 'principles of law' have been assimilated to values. Habermas is quick to point out that this is an ethical claim and as such can be effectively critiqued. The thesis is as follows: if the Constitutional Court can justify its role as one which depends on a doctrine of values, the assumption is that it can only do so authoritatively. The argument hinges on the distinction between norms and values, a distinction derived from the earlier discourse ethics. Values are conceived of as particular, historical and context-limited. Values are asserted against other values. They are not the same as norms. Habermas argues that the reconceptualization of norms as values relies on a certain conceptual confusion. Norms are obligatory while values are teleological. Above all, norms require rational justification while values refer to recommended behaviors.

> Because norms and principles, by reason of their deontological validity character, can claim to be *universally binding* and not just *specially preferred*, they possess a greater justificatory force than values; values must be brought into a transitive order with other values from case to case.[35]

Habermas's point is that norms require a procedural mechanism for rational universalization while values can only be legitimated as preferences. As a consequence, when the 'court adopts the doctrine of an objective order of values and bases its decision-making on it, the danger of irrational rulings increases, because functionalistic arguments then gain the upper hand over normative ones'.[36]

If the latter is the case this critique will yield a reconceptualization of the role of the Constitutional Court. The result of these 'methodological considerations' will be a 'critique of a false self-understanding' with regard to the role of the courts, but it does not 'deny the possibility of rationally deciding constitutional cases in general'.[37] In other words, the distinction between norms and values will lead to a reconceptualization of the role of the courts not only in relationship to its own self-understanding, but also regarding the understanding of its relation to the political legislative process. Here, Habermas relies on the distinction between justification and application.

> In any case, the constitutional judicial review initiated by individual cases is *limited* to the *application* of (constitutional) norms presupposed as valid; thus the distinction between discourses of norm application and those of norm justification offers at least an argumentation-theoretic criterion for demarcating the respective tasks that the judiciary and the legislature can legitimately accomplish.[38]

This differentiation would simultaneously define the courts' role in a procedural manner and distinguish the respective tasks of courts and legislature. At the same time it would conceive of legal adjudication on the basis of a procedural understanding of the constitution. Following J. H. Ely, Habermas would reinterpret constitutions in a procedural manner. This would mean that the constitution would be interpreted as that which 'regulates organizational and procedural problems'. The Supreme Court in turn as the interpreter of the constitution would 'look after procedures and organizational norms upon which the legitimating effect of the democratic process depends'.[39] It would follow that 'communicative and participatory rights constitutive of democratic will-formation acquire a privileged position'.[40]

The substance of this procedural argument would lead to a direct link between the activity of the courts and democratic will-formation. The problem is how to establish the link. While the liberal view short-circuits the link by concerning itself only with private autonomy, other views will associate the activity of the courts with democratic will-formation more directly. Here, Habermas introduces Frank Michelman's 'republican' view of the role of the courts in relationship to the political process. What the republican view does that the liberal cannot is to conceive of rights as something more than 'negative liberties'. The Aristotelian connotations of this view are apparent. The classic line is that politics is to be associated with the public good and grounded in the ethical activity of the citizenry. Hence, an already defined ethos of the community characterizes both its political and its legal activity. According to Habermas, the good part of this view is that it can be seen to locate rights in the public autonomy of its citizenry. But the predefined ethos of the community is seen to act as a negative governing device which ties deliberative activity to the *context* of an already given historical situation. This is of course the repetition of Habermas's critique of the communitarian perspective which, in the discourse view, has the failing that by not being able to free itself from context, it is unable to free itself sufficiently to deal with the dilemmas of modern pluralism. Further, it is unable to distinguish between politics, ethics and law radically enough to examine the question of validity from an argumentation-theoretic point of view. Habermas has a point. If one were to examine the emergence of a legal order from the point of view of an ethical standard, law that emerges from strategic interests would be undermined. Hence, this critique of republicanism is located as much on the level of facticity as on the level of validity.

> The deliberative mode of legislative practice is not just intended to ensure the ethical validity of laws. Rather, one can understand the complex validity claim of legal norms as the claim, on the one hand, to take into consideration strategically asserted particular interests in a manner compatible with the common good and, on the other hand, to bring universalistic principles of justice into the horizon of a specific form of life stamped by particular value constellations.[41]

Ultimately, the intention is not to completely undercut the 'republican' point of view, rather it is to show that there are components other than the ethical ones in legal adjudication and legislative action.

VI The deliberative paradigm

In the course of the book, Habermas has made the anti-positivistic claim that law cannot be dissociated from the implicit image of society with which it is associated. If one accepts this assumption, a second follows regarding the appropriate image of society with which law is to be associated. In the final chapter Habermas makes the case for law as viewed through the deliberative paradigm. In good Hegelian fashion it is this argument which has been operating behind our backs from the outset where the case was made, against a purely jurisprudential or philosophical perspective, for an interpretation which integrated a philosophical with a sociological or social-science orientation. Only now does the author choose to make it historical.

As we know from Thomas Kuhn, paradigm shifts occur only when a particular paradigm begins to lose its power of explanation. Thus it was only when the needs of the welfare state superimposed themselves upon the liberal paradigm that the latter began to lose its power, perpetuating a legal 'crisis'. This crisis in the interpretation of the function of the legal system could be understood as a crisis of paradigms because it generated a conflict between the supposed tasks to be fulfilled by 'formal law' generated under the old liberal paradigm and 'materialized law' fashioned to meet the utilitarian needs of the welfare state. As Habermas puts it: 'This *social transformation of law* was initially conceived as a process in which a new instrumental understanding of law, one related to social-welfare conceptions of justice, was laid over the liberal model of law, which it suppressed and finally supplanted.'[42] The result was a 'crisis in law' which can be interpreted as a crisis of paradigms. The consequent dilemma was both easy to characterize and difficult to resolve. As the categories of formal law tailored to preserve the rights of autonomous individuals gave way to the social needs of the new materialized law fashioned to meet the needs of the large bureaucracies generated by the welfare state, the emancipatory needs of the individual were undercut. On the one hand, with the welfare state, new social needs emerged, while on the other, the rights of individuals as individuals would be either suppressed or subordinated to the needs of the welfare state. In turn, this would give rise to debates over the usefulness of the constitutions and the indeterminacy of law both in Germany and in the United States. In other words, the conflict of paradigms resulted in a new legitimation crisis which Habermas wishes to resolve through the introduction of a new paradigm. As Habermas sees it, the result is the following: 'In Germany the [legal] profession seems to have two alternatives before it. It must either articulate a convincing understanding of law associated with a constitutional project adapted to complex societies or it must abandon a normative understanding of law altogether.'[43] In other words, the legitimacy problem generated is the one which has been the subject of this book, formulated in the question 'How is valid law possible?' In Habermas's view, the cost of giving up on the 'normative' understanding of law would be enormous. That 'would mean giving up the expectation that law can transform the weak force (*Kraft*) of uncoerced, intersubjectively shared convictions into a socially integrative power (*Macht*) ultimately capable of overcoming every instance of mere force (*Gewalt*), in whatever form it disguises itself'.[44] The result given the argument is to rethink the paradigm in order to see whether or not the proceduralist or deliberative paradigm can overcome the dilemma created by the current crisis.

How can certain forms of autonomy, in part the achievement of the liberal paradigm, be retained in the context of the juridification, the materialization of law, that has taken place through the superimposition of the welfare state paradigm? That is the technical way to put the question. In a more positive way, the 'desired' paradigm in question should not only 'satisfy the best description of complex societies', it should also 'illuminate the original idea of the self-constitution of a community of free and equal citizens'.[45] From the pragmatic perspective this question of the proper paradigm is not a purely theoretical question to be laid on the shoulders of those who conduct legal adjudication. Rather, as Habermas quite rightly points out, this is a political question to be decided democratically by those who participate in the political process, or at least not in their absence.

If we follow the historical argument the claim is that while the liberal model failed by conceiving the appropriate sphere of legal regulation to be associated with private autonomy too narrowly in absence of the market mechanism, the social-welfare paradigm found it necessary to 'materialize' rights but in such a way that the categories of freedom and equality which were to be protected under the liberal paradigm were marginalized. Given the prior argument of the book one could anticipate the critique: 'Both views lose sight of the internal connection between private and *civic* autonomy, and thus lose sight of the democratic meaning of a legal community's self-organization.'[46] What is left out is an adequate consideration of the subjects of law. Referring to the two views Habermas states: 'The still unresolved dispute between these two parties is focused on the determination of the factual presuppositions for the status of legal persons in their role as addressees of the legal order. These persons are autonomous, however, only in the measure that they can be understood at the same time as authors of the law to which they are subject as addressees.'[47] What both paradigms miss and what Habermas has made as a central if not *the* central argument of the book is the circular relationship between private and public autonomy. Here we discover the core of the deliberative paradigm which was already presented in the third chapter. The first principle of that argument is that the autonomy of citizens and the legitimacy of law 'refer' to each other. In a 'postmetaphysical' world 'the only legitimate law is one that emerges from the discursive opinion- and will-formation of equally entitled citizens of a state'. Put practically, citizens of a state can 'adequately exercise their public autonomy, guaranteed by the rights of democratic participation, only insofar as their private autonomy is guaranteed'. The point is that private and public autonomy reinforce each other. One might add that this referential proposition explains how valid law is possible. And this is an eminently *communicative* proposition.

> With this conception of society the burden of normative expectations in general shifts from the level of *actors'* qualities, competences, and opportunities to the level of *forms of communication* in which an informal and noninstitutionalized opinion- and will-formation is played out.[48]

From the perspective of the internal structure of the book, there is a curious circularity in the argument. As one might recall, the argument began with some methodological propositions about the nature of language which were based on forms of communication. At the end, the argument, having entered deeply into the discussion of the nature, character and legitimacy of modern law, returns to where it began with a powerful claim regarding the communicative foundation of modern law. Habermas argues that 'a legal order *is* legitimate to the extent that it equally secures the co-original private and public autonomy of its citizens'. But that can only be so because 'it *owes* its legitimacy to the forms in which alone this autonomy can express and prove itself'. If that were not enough, he adds, '*This is the key to a proceduralist understanding of law*'[49] (emphases added).

Conclusion

This is an extraordinary book. In some ways it may be Habermas's best book. For those who have followed Habermas's development over the years it represents a kind of bringing together of the various occasionally disparate strands of his work. One can trace the preoccupation with the problem of validity both to *Knowledge and Human Interests* and to *Legitimation Crisis*. The preoccupation with modes of democracy and democratization of the public sphere go back to his original work, *The Structural Transformation of the Public Sphere*. His reinterpretation of the history of law goes back to and parallels his treatment of the history of philosophy in *The Philosophical Discourse of Modernity*. Finally, he is able to make good in a public way on the thesis about communication first fully formulated in *The Theory of Communicative Action*.

There will also be critics. I would anticipate that the most potent criticisms will come from the lawyers and the philosophers. The legal profession will claim that the distinction between facticity and validity is not only much too abstract, it results in conceiving the role of the legal profession (lawyers, judges, courts and law professors) much too narrowly. If one accepts the initial proposition regarding the co-originality of private and public autonomy it would follow that judges and courts would have to submit to a higher form of rationality, a form of idealism, which would circumscribe their, very empirical, role. They will want to argue that in a democratic society the defence, interpretation and adjudication of the law by legal professionals will be far more necessary than this interpretation would allow.

Philosophers will attack the central premiss about communication which lies at the heart of the argument. They will claim that the arguments about the centrality of communication are based on certain assumptions regarding speech-act theory. If the assumptions about speech-act theory cannot be justified, how can the central thesis about communication which underlies the argument of the book be justified? Equally, moral philosophers will attack the moral (discourse) theory upon which the book is based. The liberals will want to reject the attempt to undercut the sociological critique of moral theory on the basis of claims to a more philosophical understanding of the genesis of liberal theory, while the more communitarian-minded will want to critique the attempt to de-contextualize both morality and law.

There will be other critics. However, the book promises to play a central role in the future debate on the role of law, not merely because of its theoretical contribution, which is monumental, but because its author has generated a new framework, a new architectonic, from which the phenomenon of law in a democratic society can be perceived. In that sense, this book which was written in the shadow of the great German discourses on law authored by Hegel and Weber will cast its own light.

Boston College, Massachusetts

Notes

1 Jürgen Habermas, *Faktizität und Geltung* (Frankfurt am Main: Suhrkamp, 1992), p. 18. In general I have followed the translations of William Rehg, the translator of the forthcoming text in English.
2 ibid., p. 19.
3 ibid., p. 29.
4 ibid., p. 33.
5 ibid.
6 ibid.
7 ibid., p. 44.
8 ibid., p. 51.

9   ibid., p. 81.
10   ibid., p. 96.
11   ibid., p. 101.
12   ibid., p. 110.
13   ibid., p. 109.
14   ibid., p. 133.
15   ibid., p. 135.
16   ibid., p. 143.
17   ibid., p. 157.
18   ibid., p. 169.
19   ibid., pp. 176–7.
20   ibid., p. 178.
21   ibid., p. 181.
22   ibid., p. 182.
23   ibid., p. 185.
24   ibid., p. 186.
25   ibid., p. 243.
26   ibid., p. 245.
27   ibid., p. 248.
28   ibid., p. 247.
29   ibid., p. 256.
30   ibid.
31   ibid.
32   ibid., p. 257 (quoted from R. Dworkin, *Law's Empire*, Cambridge, MA: Harvard University Press, 1986, p. 52).
33   ibid.
34   ibid., p. 264.
35   ibid., p. 315.
36   ibid., p. 316.
37   ibid., p. 317.
38   ibid., p. 318.
39   ibid., p. 321.
40   ibid.
41   ibid., p. 344.
42   ibid., p. 470.
43   ibid., p. 471.
44   ibid.
45   ibid., p. 474.
46   ibid., p. 491.
47   ibid.
48   ibid., p. 492.
49   ibid., p. 493 (emphases added).

Pierre Guibentif

Approaching the production of law through Habermas's concept of communicative action

The relations between Jürgen Habermas and the sociology of law are ambivalent. There are, on the one hand, obvious convergences between their substantive interests. A domain of common concern is, for instance, what the sociology of law usually calls the production of law. Yet, on the other hand, Habermas, by tackling the law, is moving away from sociology. And this happens precisely at a time when the sociology of law – at least in Europe – is consolidating its identity as a domain of the social sciences.[1]

Even if he assumes himself to be basically a philosopher, Habermas has often adopted the position of a sociologist. To be brief, he does this every time he plays the role of the 'stand-in', marking the place for 'empirical theories with strong universalistic claims' (Habermas, 1981c: 23). During the last few years, however, Habermas has again given precedence to his role as an interpreter, trying to mediate between our *Lebenswelt* (lifeworld) and, one of the 'differentiated moments of Reason' (p. 25), the modern law. Witnessing Habermas's attempt at a dialogue with the German and American legal cultures – 'Habermas challenges the dominant German legal science' (Merkel, 1993) – the sociologist may feel marginalized; and the sociologist of law even more so, considering the modest position that has been attributed to him or her in Habermas's reconstruction of modern law (1992a: 62–78), even if he or she must admit that this position accurately reflects the equally modest role currently played by the sociology of law.

Given this gap between the debates Habermas intends to intervene in, and the current discussions in the field of the sociology of law, the aim of this paper is to take advantage of the above-mentioned common subject-matter – the production of law – to reconnect the sociolegal concepts with Habermas's thought. This should be, for the moment, an exclusively sociolegal exercise. I try to compare the sociolegal concepts of the production of law (I) with the models that can be derived from Habermas's work (II). Insofar as this comparison leads to the adding of complements to the sociolegal models, I examine what hypotheses may be formulated grounded on these complements, and how far such hypotheses fit available research findings (III).[2]

On the other hand, I do not discuss here another issue where Habermas's concerns meet those of the sociology of law: the role of the sociology of law as one of the possible mediations between law and society, in particular in the context of law production processes. This issue deserves a broader debate which requires, actually, some evaluation of our knowledge about the production of law.

I

There is today an increasing interest, among continental sociologists of law, in the production of law.[3] This theme had been widely neglected for decades (Ferrari, 1990: xliv; Lascoumes et al., 1989: 1), probably because it had no evident relevance for the main clients of the discipline, i.e. public agencies concerned basically with implementation and effectiveness problems. Now several researches are being carried out, based in particular on the assumption that the observation of law production processes provides valuable information about the social fields where they occur (see, for example, Commaille and Hillcoat-Nalletamby, 1993), and especially about the context of the later application of the produced legal rules (e.g. Lascoumes et al., 1989; Savelsberg, 1987); or stimulated by the growing need of international comparison among national legal practices, related in particular to the European integration process (e.g. Robert, 1991; Commaille and Hillcoat-Nalletamby, 1993).

Probably because this is a recent development, the concept of production – even if it is frequently used – lacks for the moment an explicit consensual definition. For instance, no article headed 'Production of Law' is to be found in the existing dictionary of theory and sociology of law (Arnaud et al., 1993). However, a fairly precise implicit definition can be reconstructed. Several clues may help in this reconstruction. Among these are the existence of a general sociological concept of production, and the methodological affinities among existing researches which allow us to formulate a current empirical use of the concept. There is also one author who has proposed a theory of the concept, formulated presumably against what he considered as a pre-existing concept (Santos, 1985a). To a large extent, the definitions that emerge from the analysis of these three clues correspond. This entitles us to formulate a current concept, which could be qualified, using the typology of Peters (1992: 4), as an interactionist concept of the production of law. Very shortly summarized, the definition of this interactionist concept includes four elements.

(1) Law is not made by a single entity – one legislator – but is the result of the interventions of multiple social forces or actors seeking to use the law for their own purposes, opposing each other with conflicting interests in a more or less complex structural environment (the 'producing society'). Developing this element, Santos (1985a: 305) attempts to overcome a simplistic view focused on the strategies of the capital between state and civil society, arguing that there are different places where different forces or actors confront each other.

(2) Law is not an immediate result of those conflicts, but is elaborated within a differentiated sphere, a 'production apparatus' (Bourdieu, 1986: 'legal field'), whose dynamic is not directly conditioned by the social tensions in its environment. Yet as well as its environment, this apparatus is crossed by conflicts; for instance, between different legal professions (Robert, 1991: 41; Dezalay, 1993: 5), or between government departments (Commaille and Hillcoat-Nalletamby, 1993: 90).

(3) As a result of the social processes run outside and inside the apparatus, law, a 'product' in the almost industrial sense of the term, acquires a peculiar materiality – its positivity (Luhmann, 1972/1985), from now on likely to circulate and to be consumed (Santos, 1985a: 299); likely to be used for symbolic purposes (Aubert, 1966); and originating a specific social problem by its sole volume (Chevallier, 1991: 21).

(4) The processes described by the three foregoing elements are a specific feature of modern society. The fact that law has been made positive (Luhmann, 1972/1985: 'positivated') and thus can be used as a tool or a weapon by social actors has to be related with the fact that legal practice has been rationalized, notably through the differentiation of the modern legal professions (Weber; see Trubek, 1972; Eder, 1988). Even if this last element is widely bracketed by empirical research, the connection between production of law and modernity has been used in some researches where the theory of modernity provides

Communicative action and production of law

hypotheses for the interpretation of concrete processes of law production (Savelsberg, 1987). This connection has also motivated political
conclusions, such as Santos's claim for a 'postmodern law', i.e.
precisely a type of law that would no longer be defined by production
processes in the modern sense of the expression (Santos, 1989: 118).

This model has several merits. Above all, it helps the sociologist to
overcome the strong legal myth of the 'Legislator', a mysterious figure
creating laws just as God created the world. It also invites comparisons
between processes; processes which the legal science avoids comparing
– legislation, adjudication, decision – or processes which it presents as
incapable of comparison – production of law, on the one hand, and
production of news, knowledge, health, theories and so on, on the
other. But it also has at least one serious flaw: it says nothing about the
relationship between the inside and the outside of the apparatus.

This last point has been focused on by authors who have recently
attempted to launch a new concept of production of law, based on
systems theory. In the language of systems theory as shaped by
Luhmann (1984: 40), production has to be opposed to autopoiesis and
means an elaboration process which involves elements from the
outside, while autopoiesis means an elaboration process where the
elaborating system uses its own elements. In this sense, the concept of
production of law can describe, for instance, the economic system
acting on its own legal environment, trying to influence from the
outside the processes inside the legal system (Hutter, 1989). Backed by
systems theory, this concept can take advantage of several concepts
likely to grasp what may be observed on the borderline between the
legal system and other social systems, such as irritation, structural
coupling or even ultra-cyclical linkages (Luhmann, 1992; Teubner,
1991; Teubner, 1992). The hypothesis underlying these concepts is
that connections between different systems are impossible without
developing specific devices, which may be semantic (such as the
concepts of interest or of political constitution, shared by different
systems: Luhmann, 1992: 1436), or structural, such as the 'conversation circles' observed by Hutter (1989: 94).

Since authors using the interactionist concept today commonly
acknowledge the relative autonomy of the law production apparatus,
there is no such distance between the two concepts. Even so, one
difference is worth mentioning: while the interactionist concept is
associated with the model of society mainly characterized by conflicts,
the systemic concept is associated with the model of a society mainly
characterized by functional differentiation. Combinations of both
models are possible, however, as has been demonstrated by Santos
(1985a).

II

In his recent writings, Habermas himself uses several times the expression 'production of law' (Habermas, 1988: 229, 274; 1989a: 150; 1992a: 239, 241, 492), and, as a matter of fact, his attention is focused on the procedures of law elaboration, in the context of his reflections on the legitimation problem (below, point 1). Thereby, Habermas (1989b) comes back to a historical moment he had already analyzed in one of his earliest writings, 'Natural Law and Revolution' (1963/1974: 89/82): the French Revolution. In this early text, Habermas had made a first attempt to understand the role of the law in modern societies. Even if, at that moment, Habermas did not yet use the expression 'production of law', this text addresses a case of production of law: the production of the *Déclaration des droits de l'homme et du citoyen*, which made possible the production of a new legal order. 'Natural Law and Revolution' is embedded in a broader reflection on the differentiation of science and law in modern society, which leads Habermas to formulate a model of law as something modernity has made 'producible' (below, point 2).

Habermas's thought has undergone significant transformations between 'Natural Law and Revolution' (1963/1974) and 'Has the Heartbeat of the Revolution Stopped?' (1989b). The comparison between the two periods here at stake may entitle us to better identify these transformations as far as they concern the law, and may help us to better understand Habermas's current position.

1 Law and modernity

Among his other early works, it is in *Theory and Practice* that Habermas directly addresses the question of the production of law, especially – but not only – in the chapter 'Natural Law and Revolution'. His main concern in *Theory and Practice* – a collection of papers elaborated between 1961 and 1963 – is the difficulty that social sciences find in grasping an essential part of social reality, namely praxis. Habermas's central hypothesis is that this difficulty has to be related to the break, in modern societies, between scientific knowledge on the one hand, and political decision-making as well as jurisprudence on the other (Habermas, 1963/1974: 238/206).

Starting off from this hypothesis, Habermas attempts to locate the origins of the separation between social praxis and sciences of society, examining the differentiation of science and politics. In this context, although the production of law is not his main subject-matter, Habermas tackles issues tightly linked to it, since the emergence of positive law and the transformations of the social uses of positive law are essential features of the historical evolution at stake.

Roughly summarized, the evolutionary process outlined by Habermas is divided into four stages. Originally (from ancient Greece to pre-modern thinkers), knowledge of society and decision belong to the same discipline of thought, 'politics' being a part of practical philosophy (below, point a). In the second stage (Hobbes), an autonomous science of society – social philosophy – breaks away from practical philosophy (point b). In the third stage (the French Revolution, Hegel, Marx), the new science of society is reintegrated into a new normative understanding of society (point c). In the fourth stage, norm-making is differentiated from the social sciences (point d).

(a) During the first stage[4] nothing exists that could be regarded as equivalent to the production of law. To rule a society does not mean to make rules for this society, but, in consideration of pre-existing rules, which are simultaneously laws and ethical standards, to act in accordance with an adequate understanding of the social situation:

> Aristotle saw no opposition between the constitution formulated in the *nomoi* and the ethos of civil life; conversely, the ethical character of action was not separable from custom and law. (Habermas, 1963/1974: 48/42)

(b) Regarding the second stage,[5] Habermas mentions two phenomena related to the production of law; one intellectual, the other material. As an intellectual fact, the production of law is what the 'social philosophy' developed by Hobbes aims at. Social philosophy attempts to achieve a precise understanding of the natural causes of existing social rules, in order to provide the technical knowledge needed for a possible (re-)elaboration of these norms:

> It was Hobbes who studied the 'laws of civil life' with the explicit purpose of placing political action from now on on the incomparably more certain basis of that scientifically controlled technics which he had come to know in the mechanics of his time. (Habermas, 1963/1974: 66/61)

Thus, according to Habermas, the idea of the production of law, as an intellectual purpose, emerges with Hobbes. Yet this emergence is related by Habermas to several material phenomena. One of these, as it appears in the above quoted statement, is the rise of technology. A second is the existence in the United Kingdom of a '*societas*', i.e. a class of bourgeois capable of negotiating the functions of the state with the king (Habermas, 1963/1974: 62/57). Finally – and here Habermas meets the subject of the production of law on the material level – the idea of production of law becomes possible, in part, precisely because something which can be qualified as production of law has already occurred:

> ... in the meantime, the Reformation had led to a positivation[6] and formalization of the prevailing Thomistic Natural Law. ... Such formal law corresponded to objective conditions insofar as the two great processes which fundamentally changed the interconnection of *dominium* and *societas* asserted themselves within the territorial states of the sixteenth century: that is, the centralization and at the same time the bureaucratization of power within the modern state apparatus of the sovereign national governments, as well as the expansion of capitalistic trade in commodities and the gradual transformation of the mode of production, till then bound to household production. This new complex of interests of national and territorial economies ... developed under the governance [*Reglement*[7]] of a supreme authority, which was only beginning to attain full sovereignty. Thus, for the time being at least, this sphere 'of civil society', authorized by absolute rule, can be appropriately conceived in terms of the categories of the modern state, precisely the categories of a formal law technically applied to the regulation of social intercourse. (Habermas, 1963/1974: 67/62)

Hobbes's project of producing adequate laws, however, could not be translated into practical terms, because of the following antinomy (Habermas, 1963/1974: 78/74): Hobbes could intend his theory for a bourgeois public opinion in order to orient it on the way to a reorganization of society, but this theory itself negates the relevance of such a bourgeois public opinion; by explaining the citizens' actions through natural causes, it negates the citizens' autonomy of will and action. Hobbes could also address the king, to whom he could offer a technocratic guideline for the manipulation of his subjects. Yet such manipulation strategies would negate the very foundation of the royal power, which is − according to Hobbes's theory − the consent of the citizens, since this consent could not be validly given by merely manipulable subjects.

Habermas interprets the further evolution as conditioned by this antinomy, considering the next two stages as characterized by two different ways to deal with it. In a first ephemeral stage, attempts are made to integrate immediately into the political practice a social philosophy developed on the basis of Hobbes's work (third stage). Later, the practice of politics is transformed in order to secure its articulation with an empirically radicalized form of social philosophy, the social sciences, separated from praxis (fourth stage).

Communicative action and production of law

(c) The French Revolution[8] constitutes in Habermas's view an event *sui generis*, concerning the relations between theory and practice. On the one hand, the Revolution is the result of an interconnection between the social theory developed since Hobbes and political practice; it can be considered as a 'becoming practical of theory' (Habermas, 1963/1974: 131/125). Yet on the other hand, its historical unfolding demonstrates that such an immediate interconnection can no longer be maintained: the becoming practical of theory had to be 'precarious' (ibid.).

Facing the antinomy of Hobbes's social philosophy, later scholars, and among them especially the physiocrats, have completed the theory of society, providing it with a new foundation and adding to it a program for its implementation. What founds the validity of the new knowledge about society is the debate among enlightened philosophers. The theory will be implemented by the action of the monarch on the basis of the insights provided by this debate (Habermas, 1963/1974: 81/77). The 'becoming practical' of this theory occurs with the revolutionary situation when philosophers, mainly influenced by the physiocrats and by Rousseau, find themselves in charge of enlightening, no longer the monarch, but the sovereign people. The concrete medium of this enlightening is the *Déclaration des droits de l'homme et du citoyen*:

> The majority of the Assembly considered a declaration to be necessary, because the public required effectively publicized enlightenment. . . . In France [the *Déclaration*] had first to form the *opinion publique*. (Habermas, 1963/1974: 97/91).

Because they have been enlightened by the Déclaration, the representatives of the nation will be capable of deliberating valid laws. Thus, the Déclaration can be regarded as founding the new legal order:

> The French declaration . . . is intended to assert positively for the first time a fundamentally new system of rights [*soll prinzipiell neues Recht positiv erst zur Geltung bringen*[9]]. In France, the revolutionary meaning of the declaration is to lay the foundation of a new constitution. (Habermas, 1963/1974: 94/87)

This purpose appears in the Déclaration itself, which states how law ought to be produced (section 6):

> The law is the expression of the general will. All citizens are entitled to contribute personally or through their representatives, to its formation.

The precise meaning of the French Déclaration is assessed by Habermas through a comparison with the American Declaration of Independence, which 'could only have the significance of reasserting what was in any case a living common conviction' (Habermas, 1963/1974: 94/88). Thus, the American Declaration *states* a conviction, while the French Déclaration *creates* a system of rights. There are two main reasons for this difference, pointed out by Habermas. On the one hand, the Americans are influenced by the liberal thought (Locke), developed in a context (Britain) where the problem to be solved is the relationship between the monarch and an effectively functioning network of commercial relations – the *societas* already taken into consideration by Hobbes. In this context, the prevailing idea is to safeguard a natural order (already assimilated by the actors of the economy) against abusive intervention by the state. On the other hand, the concrete situations of the two countries are different. In America a new state has to be institutionalized in a land that has recently become independent. The citizens of this new state have already begun to live in accordance with their institutional projects, and the Declaration has only to formulate these. In France a new republic has to be constructed and simultaneously an old regime to be dismantled, while the concrete context remains the same. The break has to be marked symbolically by the Déclaration, which thereby creates the new social order.

In a certain sense, the French Revolution seems to fulfill the Enlightenment's project of the emancipation of man, and does it in an emblematic way in the legal field: man dominates the law. Yet, in contemporary societies, the gap between the law and man's praxis has broadened again. So the question arises: why was the immediate integration of law (as well as of social science) and praxis, experienced by the Revolution, not able to last? Paradoxically, Habermas's explanations about this last transition, between the historically most significant event and current times, are especially difficult to make out. I shall mention here only one of the explanations Habermas alludes to in *Theory and Practice*, because of its tight affinity to Habermas's recent reflections, to be discussed below. This explanation is suggested to Habermas by Hegel:

> The direct actualization of the abstract Right [*abstraktes Recht*] that has been outlined in theory, presents the problem of mediating a simple, unbending, cold generality with the absolute brittleness and obstinate punctiliousness of self-consciousness as it exists in reality. But as both of these extremes have been extracted from the continuity of the practical interrelationships of life [*praktischer Lebenszusammenhang*] and thus are absolute, for themselves, relationship

between them can 'send out no part towards the middle by which they could link up'. The revolutionary activity authorized by subjective consciousness is therefore the negation of the individual in the general. Its sole work is death and indeed 'the coldest most insipid death, with no more significance than chopping through a head of cabbage or gulping down water'. (Habermas, quoting Hegel, 1963/1974: 132/ 125)

In later texts, Habermas (1971) explicitly adopts this reasoning on the basis of the necessary separation of theory-building and enlightenment, on the one hand, and political will-formation (1971: 38) and strategic activity (1971: 41),[10] on the other. His most synthetical statement in this sense is the following:

> Organization of enlightenment and strategic activity are two different things and cannot be implemented *uno actu*. (Habermas, 1972: 327)

(d) Just as if history would have learned from Hegel's advice, science of society as well as political decision will withdraw from the realm of the 'practical interrelationships of life' soon after the revolutionary experience:[11]

> Now this constellation of dogmatism, reason and decision (that characterizes the Enlightenment) has changed profoundly since the eighteenth century, and exactly to the degree to which positive sciences have become productive forces in social development. For as our civilization has become increasingly scientific, the dimension within which theory was once directed toward praxis has been correspondingly strangled [*zugeschnürt*].[12] . . . In this system, science, technology, industry and administration interlock a circular process. In this process the relationship of theory to praxis can only assert itself as the purposive-rational application of techniques assured by empirical science. (Habermas, 1963/1974: 308/254)

Referring here to the administration, Habermas addresses one of the two ways of producing law developed in modern societies. Law is elaborated on the basis of merely empirical data regarding the means and effects of the decisions (see also Habermas, 1964), not the values that inspire the goals they aim at. The other way of producing law is advocated by certain legal theorists who draw a more radical conclusion from the revolutionary experience. They argue that, apart from any rational or empirical foundations, decisions can be validated only by the mere will of who decides:

> *Decisionism* as a world-view today is no longer ashamed to reduce norms to decisions. . . . Such decisions then can be interpreted . . . in a

public, political sense (Carl Schmitt) . . . the thesis remains the same: that decisions relevant to the praxis of life . . . are not accessible to rational consideration and cannot form a rationally substantiated consensus. (Habermas, 1963/1974: 319/266)

So the law production apparatus built up in the course of the revolutionary period has become autonomous in relation to its genuine support: the community of the citizens. A closure has occurred, which can assume the radical feature of a dogmatic closure: political jurists consider themselves as the only legitimate producers of law, on the basis of decisionism. In other cases, we may speak about a technocratical closure: the foundations no longer supplied by public debate, but by the empirical results of science run under state instructions.

2 Legitimation and communication

Since the linguistic turn, one of the main concerns of Habermas is the problem pointed out by the terms 'legitimacy' and 'legitimation'[13] which is addressed in almost all Habermas's writings since the early 1970s. Two texts are emblematic: *Legitimation Crisis* (Habermas, 1973/1976) and 'How is Legitimacy possible on the Basis of Legality?' (Lecture 1 of *Law and Morality*, Habermas, 1988: 219), a translation of 'Wie ist Legitimität durch Legalität möglich?'.

Habermas meets the notion of legitimacy by elaborating his general communicative model of social activity. According to this model, concrete human interaction can work only under the condition that the participants behave just as if (*Unterstellung*) they would run a ideal speech-situation or a situation of ideal communicative action. In an early paper (Habermas, 1970/1971: 124) this ideal situation is described as requiring the two following expectations: first, we expect other people to comply *intentionally* with the rules they are obeying; second, we expect other people to comply only with those rules they accept as justified. This second expectation is called by Habermas the *legitimacy expectation*:

> This *legitimacy expectation* includes the assumption, that only such norms can be considered as justified, about which [the others] are convinced that they would – if necessary – stand up to an unlimited and unrestricted discussion. (Habermas, 1970/1971: 124)

This model grounds Habermas's basic hypothesis concerning the emergence of normativity. This hypothesis can be formulated in the following terms: since communicative interaction presupposes the legitimacy expectation, the continuance of this interaction means the

Communicative action and production of law

shared acknowledgement of norms, whether this acknowledgement is the result of an actual discussion, or is presumed because no discussion has been initiated by one of the involved parties. Thereby, communication produces legitimacy.

Taking part in the debate about the crisis of capitalist society, Habermas (e.g. 1973/1976) has to apply this hypothesis on the level of macro societies, questioning in particular the legitimation – strategies of legitimacy production – of legal norms. On this level, two problems have to be discussed. On the one hand, how is it possible to organize on a large scale a communicative activity likely to validate social norms? On the other hand, Habermas tries to explain how, in certain societies, though there is some kind of public debate, norms are legitimated that hurt the interests, of large groups of the population. How can debate legitimate unjust norms?

Chronologically, Habermas meets these two problems in the reverse order. As a matter of fact, it seems to have been the historical situation of the non-violent reproduction of unjust social relations – actually observed in the 'extreme case of the periphery' – that has drawn his attention to the problem of legitimation as well as to the communicative dimension of it. Habermas considers that such situations should be analyzed on the basis of the main hypotheses of *The Structural Transformation of the Public Sphere*, revisited by a theory of communicative action:

> The phenomenon we have to explain consists in the effective establishing of an appearance of justification that provides existing institutions with a non-violent acknowledgement. I try to explain this structural violence through the systematic limitations of will-forming discourses. (Habermas, 1972: 319)

In Habermas's more recent papers, this question of legitimation systems as structural violence gives precedence to the broader question of the conditions of a legitimative public discourse. This question leads Habermas to the issue, raised by Luhmann (1969), of legitimation through procedure.[14] His approach to this issue suffers a remarkable evolution during the period here at stake. It starts with a global refusal of Luhmann's hypothesis:

> The organs of legislation and adjudication certainly are not legitimated through the way they proceed, but through a general interpretation, that backs the domination system as a whole. (Habermas in Habermas and Luhmann, 1971: 244; see also Habermas, 1981a: Vol. 1, 358)

To a certain extent, Habermas withdraws from this position in *The Theory of Communicative Action*:

> In the face of a changing and steadily increasing volume of positive law, modern legal subjects content themselves in actual practice with legitimation through procedure, for in many cases substantive justification is not only not possible, but is also, from the viewpoint of the lifeworld, meaningless. This is true of all cases where the *law* serves as a *means for organizing media-controlled subsystems* which have, in any case, become autonomous vis-a-vis the normative contexts of action oriented towards reaching understanding. (Habermas, 1981d/ 1986: 536/212)

So part of positive law – the positive law needed for the functioning of the systems – may be legitimized through procedures, while another part – the domain of the core principles of our legal orders – needs 'a material justification' (ibid.).[15] This distinction has not been discussed again in more recent papers, possibly because Habermas has 'generally left the "systems" to the "system theorists"' (Peters, 1992: 35), but probably also because, instead of refuting Luhmann's idea of legitimation through procedure, Habermas tries now to make it acceptable by shaping the criteria of an adequate procedure.

As a first step, Habermas suggests that legal procedures may provide legitimacy because they can be – and, to a certain extent, he assumes they actually are – connected with our experience of communicative action, for they rely upon similar standards:[16]

> Legitimacy is possible on the basis of legality insofar as the procedures for the production and application of legal norms are also conducted reasonably, in the moral practical sense of procedural rationality. (Habermas, 1988: 230)

This first criterion will be complemented soon by a second one, elaborated by Habermas following his papers of 1989 (1989a, 1989b). What is likely to produce legitimation on a macro-social level is the fact that public procedures are run on two distinct levels: through 'legally constituted political will-formation' procedures, on the one hand, and in the 'communicative flows of autonomous public spheres' on the ·other (Habermas, 1989a: 154). The distinction between these two levels has become central in all Habermas's recent political writings.[17] Interestingly, it corresponds both to Habermas's own earlier concerns about the distinction between the Enlightenment and political activity (see above, point 1c), and to certain basic assumptions of the systemic theory of law developed by Luhmann and Teubner.[18]

This distinction is the core element of the normative theory of law presently developed by Habermas. What is at stake is to explain why this distinction has to be maintained, and to identify how both spheres have to be articulated in order to assure a legitimate production of law.

Regarding the first question, the reasoning of Habermas may be analyzed in two complementary considerations. On the one hand, the distinction between the two levels allows a 'division of labour'. The legal discourse defines the limited set of social norms which may ground enforceable claims, and institutionalizes the 'organized bodies' (Habermas, 1989a: 154) which can produce such norms and those which are responsible for the application of such norms (Habermas, 1992a: 141). Discourses in the autonomous public spheres supply the production and application discourses with arguments, while formulating social needs and defining what issues are relevant at a given moment (Habermas, 1989a: 154; 1989b: 31). On the other hand, the distinction between legalized procedures and informal debates in the autonomous public spheres is the very mechanism that produces the imperativity of modern law. Public debates produce 'communicative power' which is 'transformed into administrative power' by law (Habermas, 1992a: 235; see also p. 187). Thereby, modern law is able to

> . . . transform the weak force of unconstrainedly by formed, intersubjectively shared convictions in a social-integrative power, which is ultimately able to dominate all kinds of naked violence. (ibid., p. 471)

Yet the apparatus constituted by these two distinct spheres can produce legitimate norms only if an appropriate articulation between both spheres is ensured. On the side of the autonomous public spheres, this means that sensitive issues have to be intensively discussed, and the terms of these discussions publicized so that they cannot be ignored by those who are in charge of the formal procedures:

> Communicative power is used on the mode of the besiegement. It influences the premises of processes of adjudication and decision without any attempt to conquest, invoking their imperatives in the only language that can be understood by the besieged[19] fortress: it manages the pool of reasons that can be handled by the administration, which is unable – since legally constituted – to ignore them. (Habermas, 1989b: 31)

On the side of the legally organized will-formation processes, the participants have to 'remain open and sensitive to those communicative flows of autonomous public sphere' (Habermas, 1989a: 154). This is especially an obligation of those who as professionals are entitled to the social use of the law. They will have to develop a conception of their legal practice – a 'legal paradigm' (Habermas, 1992a: 238, 527) – that fits the urgent need of articulation between legal procedures and public debate. This new legal paradigm should be procedural, challenging both pre-existing conflicting paradigms, the liberal paradigm and the welfare state paradigm (ibid.: 480, 505).[20] Contributing to the development of this new legal paradigm, this is what Habermas aims at in – and through[21] – *Faktizität und Geltung* (1992a: 493).

Habermas has had the opportunity to put his theory of legitimation through communication into practice during the German unification process. In a newspaper article (1990b), he advocated that the unification should be the result of a constitutional reform which would have required a large public debate. Only such a debate, he argued, would have supplied the conditions for the regeneration of the autonomous public spheres in the former GDR and provided the administrative implementation of the unification with the necessary normative parameters. By publishing this article, Habermas was intervening in the autonomous public sphere constituted by the readership of the left-liberal weekly newspaper *Die Zeit*, basing his intervention on an interpretation of the German *Grundgesetz*, an interpretation oriented by a procedural legal paradigm. This proposition has not been considered by the government. The legal basis on which unification was achieved required only the decision, on the part of the eastern *Länder*, to join the FRG, as well as a parliamentary debate. This is now related by Habermas to the current problems faced by Germany, in particular right-wing extremism in the former GDR and the violence against asylum-seekers. The way the unification process has been run, no public sphere could emerge in the eastern *Länder* (Habermas, 1992c), and the normative structures within the autonomous public spheres in Germany have been weakened, rendering questionable the legitimacy even of the *Grundgesetz* itself, in the eyes not only of the population, but also of the politicians (Habermas, 1992d).

This public intervention shows that, according to Habermas, the mechanism of the legitimation through the separation and articulation between legally organized processes and autonomous public spheres is not only a goal for legal politics, but also, to a certain extent, a reality likely to explain, *hic et nunc*, legitimation strategies and legitimacy shortages.

Communicative action and production of law

III

Bringing together the two stages of reflection outlined above, it is possible now to delineate Habermas's concept of the production of law and its main transformations. This can be done in four points. (1) Law as something that can be produced is a modern phenomenon. Production of law was practised for a first exemplary occasion during the French Revolution; the complex apparatus required for the continuance of this production has emerged with the differentiation of complex modern societies. (2) Producing law is a matter of communication. It was the intuition of the philosophers and politicians involved in the French Revolution. It is why Habermas has since the beginning rejected the decisionist legal theory. It is the key, now supplied by the theory of communicative action, completed with the theory of the communicative power, which Habermas uses to interpret the role of public debates in modern states. (3) Legitimate law can only be produced when the sphere of legal procedures has been differentiated from the sphere of autonomous public debates. That is why historically the production of law has withdrawn from the praxis. This is what Habermas observes today, accepting it as a necessity and taking it into account by intervening as an intellectual in German public debates. (4) Among other factors, the production of law is conditioned by the attitudes of the professionals of law, and these attitudes may vary throughout the universe of legal culture. This is a phenomenon Habermas discovered during the second stage described above, especially during the last years he has dedicated most of his attention to the internal aspects of the legal culture.

If we compare this concept of the production of law with those currently used by sociologists of law, we may bring out (1) correspondences and (2) complements suggested by Habermas's contribution to the sociology of law, as well as (3) interrogations, arising from the sociological concepts, addressed to Habermas.

1 Theory confirming the empirical

Habermas's reflections are converging with sociological observations on three significant points: the existence of a differentiated society as the background of law production processes, also assumed by the systemic model (even if on that point there are differences between Habermas's and the interactionist models, to be shortly discussed below); the differentiation of the law as an autonomous social sphere, which is assumed both by the interactionist and the systemic model; and the relevance of the tensions inside the legal culture for the production of law, which has been observed in the course of several empirical investigations. These convergences are worth emphasizing. Because Habermas draws his conclusions from processes which differ radically from sociological observation as well as from systematic theory-building, these conclusions can be considered not simply as corresponding to, but as reinforcing the current conclusions of sociological work.

There is an obvious, less significant point of convergence, which is the connection of production of law with modernity. It is less significant because to some extent the sociolegal reflection on that point has developed on the basis of (Eder, 1988) or against (Raes, 1986) Habermas's thought.

2 Possible developments for the sociology of law

The main challenge Habermas's concept addresses to the sociology of law is the connection between legitimacy and communication. Empirical research on the production of law obviously deals with communication (analysis of the media, minutes of commissions, parliamentary debates, etc.), but focuses on the contents, generally neglecting to take the performative aspects into account. And there are few attempts to connect the observations gathered on the level of the debates with observations related to the acceptance of law. Furthermore, as a whole, the question of legitimation remains marginal in researches about the production of law, partly because it is merged with the observance and effectiveness issues other researches are dealing with. These limitations of the research on the production of law could partly be explained as related to the 'industrialist' connotations of the expression 'production of law', which has led, for instance, to the abusive metaphor of the 'machine of production of law'. This metaphor, obviously, brackets the communicative element in the elaboration of the law, just as the distinction between production and consumption suggests a sharp-separation between the elaboration and the application processes.

Following the suggestion of Habermas, research designs should be developed joining observations of the production process of legal norms with observations of their application, in order to confirm empirically the links between discussions surrounding the production and attitudes in the application contexts. For the moment, one example could illustrate the relevance of the general hypothesis of the legitimation through communication.

Several authors (Santos, 1985b: 883; Dauderstädt, 1988: 444; Beleza, 1990: 680) consider that so-called semi-peripheral countries are characterized by an extremely large gap between law and social practices. Obviously, formulated in these terms, this statement is methodologically questionable: it raises the question whether there is a qualitative difference between the gap observed in such countries and the gap between 'law in the books' and 'law in action' in central countries: it ignores differences between the various legal domains; and so on. But indeed the statement fits numerous observations which may be collected in such countries, so that it seems acceptable to use it at least for the sake of the present reasoning. Assuming that there is such a gap between law and society in semi-peripheral countries, which can be formulated in terms of a lack of legitimacy, the hypothesis here at stake focuses our attention on the spheres of public discussion of legal issues, and on the mediations between those spheres and the formal legal procedures. Deficiencies observed in those realms could be interpreted as explanatory factors of the legitimacy shortage.

Taking Portugal as an example, there are indeed several research findings already available pointing out such deficiencies. Reform processes in highly sensitive matters such as family and divorce law (Barbosa et al., 1993: 28) are hardly commented on in the newspapers. There are almost no special sections of the newspapers devoted to legal issues. The press has no access to significant parts of the formal will-formation processes, such as, for instance, the debates of the commission in charge of the elaboration of the draft for constitutional reform (Miranda et al., 1986: 56). The popular level of information about law is extremely low due to the fact that there is no regularly updated organized law collection.

Institutionalized mediations are weak: rules concerning the consultation of the main consultative body, the Conselho Económico e Social, by the government, which produces the largest part of the legislation, are elusive (Marques and Ferreira, 1991: 36). Finally, within the legal sphere itself, there is little space for debate. A strongly legalistic understanding of the courts' activity narrows the scope for judicial argumentation (Hespanha, 1986: 326; Beleza, 1990: 679). No legal journal and no association can be considered as mediating among the different legal professions (Guibentif, 1989: 161), so that there is no locus for broad debates on legally relevant issues, and, using Habermas's concept, for the emergence of national legal paradigms. Confirming the constraints faced by reflective efforts within the legal sphere, the sociology of law has had to develop almost completely disconnected from the law schools (Beleza, 1990).

Thus, there is evidence likely to consolidate the hypothesis which can be derived from Habermas's theory of legitimation through procedures. In a country where the global legitimacy of the legal system is weak, we observe that public debates on legal issues are rare and conducted under precarious conditions. Obviously, this should not lead to the conclusion that a shortage of public debate is the only cause of a shortage of legitimacy. But it allows us to admit that it constitutes a significant factor. On the basis of this general statement, it is worth examining what is the concrete weight of this factor in relation to specific issues. For instance, targeted improvements of the conditions for the public debate could be experienced, whose results should be measured on the level of the application contexts. A promising field could be the welfare legislation, whose application still follows, for a significant part, patterns shaped by the former authoritarian regime (Santos, 1991: 34).[22]

3 Question to Habermas

Though there are no sharp discrepancies between Habermas's concept and the sociological ones, there is one difference at least. In his recent writings, Habermas insists on the 'fluidity' (1989a: 154), the 'dilution' (1989b: 31) of the autonomous public spheres, which seems to negate the relevance of broader social trends on this level (in this sense, see Habermas, 1992a: 492). On the other hand, the interactionist concept of the production of law emphasizes the importance of social forces in the environment of the legal sphere, referring to the role of large social movements, to struggles between potent actors, which can be duly identified, even if these forces and actors do not act directly on the legal transformations but through different mediation devices. In this sense, a large drug industry influences patent legislation (Hutter, 1989). Recent transformations of business law can be related to the strategies of 'economic interest groupings' acting as 'transnational operators' (Dezalay, 1993: 4). The process of reforming Portuguese family law can be interpreted mainly as a struggle between the Catholic Church and left-wing political movements inspired in particular by the Communist Party (Barbosa et al., 1993: 35).

As a matter of fact, Habermas's own recent considerations are not that distant from these findings. The existence of the two competing legal paradigms he observes – the liberal paradigm and the welfare state paradigm (Habermas, 1992a: 480, 505) – certainly could be related, even if this may sound simplistic, to the existence of highly organized opposing social forces in Germany: the two dominant political forces (conservative-liberal coalition and Social Democrats); entrepreneurial lobbies, trade unions, professionals of welfare services, etc. How tight the links between the two currently dominant legal paradigms and those social forces are is an empirical question that may remain open for the moment. But admitting that there are some links, another question arises: what social forces and actors are likely to back the development of the third legal paradigm, the procedural legal paradigm?[23] From a sociological point of view, much of the practicability of the way of improving modern law suggested by Habermas depends on that question. It is a question that should, in any case, be included in the agenda of the dialogue between Habermas and the sociology of law.

Instituto Superior de Ciências do Trabalho e da Empresa,
Lisbon, Portugal

Notes

This paper was produced with the support of grants from the Goethe-Institut (Lisbon) and the Sociology Department of the ISCTE (Lisbon). I would also like to thank Peter Fitzpatrick for his stimulating critique, and Karin Wall for helping to correct my English.

1 This evolution is revealed notably by the intensification of the relations between sociological theory and empirical research. See, for instance, in Germany the connections between, among others, Hutter (1989) and Teubner, or in France between, among others, Dezalay (1993) and Bourdieu. It can be considered both as a prerequisite and an effect of the increasing international cooperation in the field. See the creation of the International Institute for the Sociology of Law (Oñati).

2 Similarly, Peters (1992: 21) considers that Habermas 'provides important hypotheses' that have to be 'supported by additional evidence'.

3 The question remains how far the issue designated to continental sociologists by the expression 'production of law' has an exact counterpart for observers of the common law legal culture, and whether the differences between 'production of law' and 'law-making' are sufficiently relevant to legitimate the use of the Latin expression in an anglo-saxon sociolegal context. This question would deserve a specific discussion between observers of both the common law and the continental legal culture.

4 Discussed at the beginning of 'The Classical Doctrine of Politics in Relation to Social Philosophy', a paper originally presented December 1961 (Habermas, 1963/1974: 48/41).

5   Central issue of 'The Classical Doctrine of Politics in Relation to Social Philosophy' (Habermas 1963/1974: 48/41; see note 4).

6   It may be interesting to note that Habermas is already using the expression 'positivation of natural law', before the expression 'positivation of law' had been introduced in the sociolegal language by Niklas Luhmann's detailed discussion of the concept, since 1966 (Luhmann, 1966: 95). See also Luhmann, 1969: 141 and 1972/1985: Part IV.

7   The original German expression has been added when the existing English translation does not entirely render the connotations of the original.

8   See 'Between Philosophy and Science: Marxism as Critique' (December 1960; Habermas, 1963/1974: 228/195); 'Hegel's Critique of the French Revolution' (July 1962; Habermas, 1963/1974: 128/121); 'Natural Law and Revolution' (October 1962; Habermas, 1963/1974: 89/82).

9   Interestingly, the translation of *Recht* by the expression 'system of rights' anticipates the recent introduction, by Habermas himself (1992a: 109;185), of the concept of *System der Rechte* in his reconstruction of modern law.

10   The expression 'strategic activity' had not, at that time, the sense that has been shaped as Habermas developed his theory of communicative action (see Habermas, 1981a: Vol. I, 62).

11   See 'Dogmatism, Reason and Decision: on Theory and Praxis in our Scientific Civilization' (1963; Habermas, 1963/1974: 307/253).

12   John Viertel's translation at this point is 'has become correspondingly constructed'. The highly metaphorical language of Habermas here is indeed difficult to understand, but this translation certainly does not fit the sense of the original text.

13   Even if the reflections of Habermas during the former period are often linked to the problem of legitimacy, there is a radical renewal of the issue with the changes of the late 1960s. A sign among others of this renewal: 'Legitimacy' is not referred to as an item in the subject index of the original German edition of Habermas (1962/1989).

14   For a broader discussion of the procedure as an issue for Habermas and for social theory in general, see Peters (1991: 227).

15   This distinction is introduced in *The Theory of Communicative Action* with the aim of explaining the differential effects of the historical process of legalization. Considering that the problem of legalization is more likely to be related to the sociolegal reflection on the impact of law, I shall not examine it here further.

16   On this aspect of Habermas's theory of law, see García Amado (1992).

17 See, e.g., Habermas (1992b: 84). For an early formulation, see Habermas (1988: 244).
18 There are, actually, several crucial references made to Luhmann in the texts where Habermas shapes his principle of the necessary distinction between formal legal procedures and their communicative environment (Habermas, 1988: 251; 1989b: 26, 36).
19 Meanwhile, Habermas (1992a: 531) has partially withdrawn from the metaphor of the 'besiegement', which he uses also in 1990a: 44.
20 A conflict that Habermas has witnessed for years, since it can already be observed in the Forsthoff–Abendroth controversy to which Habermas refers on several occasions (1988: 233; 1990a: 26; 1992a: 470).
21 As an example of the public impact of *Faktizität und Geltung*, one could mention the explicit reference made to the book in the newspaper article by Darnstädt and Spörl (1993: 135, 148).
22 See also the renewal of effectiveness research advocated by Teubner (1992). Considering this articulation between norm production and application processes, to whose restoration Habermas's concept contributes in the sociological model of law, I do not agree with Tushnet (1988: 948) when he considers – taking as his example the concept of rationalization – that Habermas's concepts are 'inaccurate in describing the law in action'.
23 In a similar sense, see Teubner's critique (1991: 27): 'if we do not take sober account of their rootedness in real social processes . . . then we are likely to let our pluralist micro-bodies decay into the "talking shops" that democratically conceived institutions have already been denounced as in our century.' See also Raes (1986: 203).

Bibliography

Arnaud, André-Jean, Belley, Jean-Guy, Carty, J. Anthony, Chiba, Masaji, Commaille, Jacques, Devillé, Anne, Landowski, Eric, Ost, François, Perrin, Jean-François, van der Kerchove, Michel and Wróblewski, Jerzy (1993) *Dictionnaire encyclopédique de théorie et de sociologie du droit.* Paris: LGDJ.

Aubert, Vilhelm (1966) 'Some Social Functions of Legislation', *Acta Sociologica* 10: 98.

Barbosa, Maria Cristina, Guibentif, Pierre, Machado, Maria Cristina and Sobral, Paula (1993) 'La production du droit de la filiation au Portugal'. Presented at the meeting of the *Réseau de recherche sur le droit de la famille en Europe* (CEVIPOF–CNRS/FNSP), Brussels.

Beleza, Tereza Pizarro (1990) 'Sociology of Law in Portugal', in Ferrari (1990), pp. 661–85.

Bourdieu, Pierre (1986) 'La force du droit. Eléments pour une sociologie du champ juridique', *Actes de la recherche en sciences sociales* (Paris, no. 64): 3.

Chevallier, Jacques (1991) 'La rationnalisation de la production juridique', in Charles-Albert Morand (ed.) *L'Etat propulsif*, pp. 11–48. Paris: Publisud.

Commaille, Jacques and Hillcoat-Nalletamby, Sarah (1993) 'Le modèle français de production de la loi'. Presented at the meeting of the *Réseau de recherche sur le droit de la famille en Europe* (CEVIPOF–CNRS/FNSP), Brussels.

Darnstädt, Thomas and Spörl, Gerhard (1993) 'Streunende Hunde im Staat', in *Spiegel Spezial – Die Erde 2000. Wohin sich die Menschheit entwickelt*, p. 128. Hamburg (special issue of *Der Spiegel*, weekly).

Dauderstädt, Michael (1988) 'Schwacher Staat und schwacher Markt: Portugals Wirtschaftspolitik zwischen Abhängigkeit und Modernisierung', *Politische Vierteljahresschrift* 29 (Opladen, Germany): 433.

Dezalay, Yves (1993) 'Multinationales de l'expertise et "dépérissement" de l'Etat', *Actes de la recherche en sciences sociales* (Paris, nos. 96/7): 3.

Eder, Klaus (1988) 'Critique of Habermas's Contribution to the Sociology of Law', *Law & Society Review* 22: 931.

Ferrari, Vincenzo, ed. (1990) *Developing Sociology of Law – A World-Wide Documentary Enquiry*. Milan: Giuffrè.

García Amado, Juan Antonio (1992) 'Justicia, democracia y validez del Derecho en Jürgen Habermas', *Sistema* (Madrid, no. 107): 115.

Guibentif, Pierre (1989) 'Rechtskultur und Rechtsproduktion. Das Beispiel Portugal', *Zeitschrift für Rechtssoziologie* 10 (Opladen, Germany): 149.

Habermas, Jürgen (1962/1989) *The Structural Transformation of the Public Sphere*. Cambridge/MA: MIT Press, 1989. (First German edition: *Strukturwandel der Öffentlichkeit: Untersuchungen zu einer Kategorie der bürgerlichen Gesellschaft*. Darmstadt/Neuwied: Luchterhand, 1962; most recent edition, with a new preface, see Habermas, 1990a.)

Habermas, Jürgen (1963/1974) *Theory and Practice*. Translated by J. Viertel. London: Heinemann, 1974. (First German edition: *Theorie und Praxis. Sozialphilosophische Studien*. Neuwied/Berlin: Luchterhand, 1963. Quoted here from the 4th German edition, to which Habermas added several more recent texts: see Habermas, 1971.)

Habermas, Jürgen (1964) 'Verwissenschaftlichte Politik und öffentliche Meinung', in *Technik und Wissenschaft als 'Ideologie'*, pp. 120–45. Frankfurt: Suhrkamp, 1969. (First issued 1964.)

Habermas, Jürgen (1970a) *Zur Logik der Sozialwissenschaften.* Frankfurt: Suhrkamp. (Quoted from the new edition, 1982.)

Habermas, Jürgen (1970/1971) 'Vorlesungen zu einer sprachtheoretischen Grundlegung der Soziologie', in Habermas (1984), pp. 11–126 (years of elaboration see ibid.: 11).

Habermas, Jürgen (1971) 'Einleitung zur Neuausgabe – Einige Schwierigkeiten beim Versuch, Theorie und Praxis zu vermitteln', in Habermas, *Theorie und Praxis.* Frankfurt: Suhrkamp. (New edition of Habermas, 1963/1974.)

Habermas, Jürgen (1972) 'Die Utopie des guten Herrschers', *Merkur* 26: 1266 (Here quoted from the new edition in Habermas (1981b), pp. 318–27.)

Habermas, Jürgen (1973/1976) *Legitimation Crisis.* Translated by T. McCarthy. London: Heinemann, 1976. (First German edition, *Legitimationsprobleme im Spätkapitalismus.* Frankfurt: Suhrkamp, 1973.)

Habermas, Jürgen (1981a) *Theorie des kommunikativen Handelns*, 2 vols. Frankfurt: Suhrkamp. (Translated by T. McCarthy, as *The Theory of Communicative Action.* Boston, MA: Beacon Press 1984, 1987.)

Habermas, Jürgen (1981b) *Kleine politische Schriften I–IV.* Frankfurt: Suhrkamp.

Habermas, Jürgen (1981c) 'Die Philosophie als Platzhalter oder Interpret', in Habermas (1983), pp. 9–28. (Conference held 1981; translated as 'Philosophy as Stand-In and Interpreter', in K. Baynes, J. Bohman and T. McCarthy (eds) *After Philosophy: End or Transformation?* Cambridge, MA: MIT Press, 1987, pp. 296–315.)

Habermas, Jürgen (1981d/1986) 'Law as Medium and Law as Institution', in Gunther Teubner (ed.) *Dilemmas of Law in the Welfare State*, pp. 203–20. Berlin/New York: De Gruyter. (Separate translation by I. Fraser and C. Meldrum of Habermas (1981a), pp. 522–47.)

Habermas, Jürgen (1983) *Moralbewusstsein und kommunikatives Handeln.* Frankfurt: Suhrkamp. (Translated as *Moral Consciousness and Communicative Action.* Cambridge, MA: MIT Press, 1990.)

Habermas, Jürgen (1984) *Vorstudien und Ergänzungen zur Theorie des kommunikativen Handelns.* Frankfurt: Suhrkamp.

Habermas, Jürgen (1988) 'Law and Morality', in Sterling M. McMurrin (ed.) *The Tanner Lectures on Human Values*, Vol. VIII, pp. 219–79. Salt Lake City/Cambridge: University of Utah Press/Cambridge University Press.

Habermas, Jürgen (1989a) 'Towards a Communication-Concept of Rational Collective Will-Formation. A Thought-Experiment', *Ratio Juris* 2: 144.

Habermas, Jürgen (1989b) 'Ist der Herzschlag der Revolution zum Stillstand gekommen?' in Forum für Philosophie Bad Homburg (ed.) *Die Ideen von 1789 in der deutschen Rezeption*, pp. 7–36. Frankfurt: Suhrkamp.

Habermas, Jürgen (1990a) 'Vorwort zur Neuauflage 1990', in *Strukturwandel der Öffentlichkeit: Untersuchungen zu einer Kategorie der bürgerlichen Gesellschaft*. Frankfurt: Suhrkamp. (First edition: see Habermas, 1962/1989, pp. 11–50.)

Habermas, Jürgen (1990b) 'Der DM-Nationalismus', *Die Zeit*, p. 62. (Hamburg, weekly, 30 March.)

Habermas, Jürgen (1992a) *Faktizität und Geltung*. Frankfurt: Suhrkamp.

Habermas, Jürgen (1992b) 'Bemerkungen zu einer verworrenen Diskussion. Was bedeutet "Aufarbeitung der Vergangenheit" heute?' *Die Zeit*, p. 82. (Hamburg, weekly, 3 April.)

Habermas, Jürgen (1992c) 'Une union sans valeur' (interview), *Liber: Revue européenne des livres* (Paris, June), p. 16.

Habermas, Jürgen (1992d) 'Die zweite Lebenslüge der Bundesrepublik: Wir sind wieder "normal" geworden', *Die Zeit*, p. 48. (Hamburg, weekly, 11 December.)

Habermas, Jürgen and Luhmann, Niklas (1971) *Theorie der Gesellschaft oder Sozialtechnologie – Was leistet die Systemforschung*. Frankfurt: Suhrkamp.

Hespanha, António Manuel (1986) 'As transformações revolucionárias e o discurso dos juristas', *Revista Crítica de Ciências Sociais* (Coimbra, nos. 18/19/20): 311.

Hutter, Michael (1989) *Die Produktion von Recht. Eine selbstreferentielle Theorie der Wirtschaft, angewandt auf den Fall des Arzneimittelpatentrechts*. Tübingen: Mohr (Siebeck).

Lascoumes, P., Roth, R. and Sansonetti, R. (1989) *L'incrimination en matière économique. Trois exemples de processus: cartels, petit crédit, initiés*. Geneva: Travaux CETEL no. 34.

Luhmann, Niklas (1966) 'Reflexive Mechanismen', in *Soziologische Aufklärung*, pp. 92–112. Opladen: Westdeutscher Verlag 1970. (First issued 1966: *Soziale Welt* 17: 1.)

Luhmann, Niklas (1969) *Legitimation durch Verfahren*. Darmstadt: Luchterhand.

Luhmann, Niklas (1972/1985) *A Sociological Theory of Law*. London/ Boston: Routledge & Kegan Paul. (Translation of the 2nd edition of *Rechtssoziologie*. Opladen: Westdeutscher Verlag, 1983. First edition, Reinbek bei Hamburg: Rowohlt, 1972.)

Luhmann, Niklas (1984) *Soziale Systeme. Grundriss einer allgemeinen Theorie*. Frankfurt: Suhrkamp.

Luhmann, Niklas (1992) 'Operational Closure and Structural Coupling:

The Differentiation of the Legal System', *Cardozo Law Review* 13: 1419.

Marques, Maria Manuel Leitão and Ferreira, António Casimiro (1991) 'A Concertação Económica e Social: A Construção do Diálogo Social em Portugal', *Revista Crítica de Ciências Sociais* (Coimbra, no. 31): 11.

Merkel, Reinhard (1993) 'Was ist das Recht?' (review of Habermas, 1992a), *Die Zeit*, p. 57. (Hamburg, weekly, 12 February.)

Miranda, Jorge, Rebelo de Sousa, Marcelo and Tavares de Almeida, Marta, eds (1986) *A Feitura das Leis*, 2 vols. Oeiras: INA.

Peters, Bernhard (1991) *Rationalität, Recht und Gesellschaft*. Frankfurt: Suhrkamp.

Peters, Bernhard (1992) 'Between System and Lifeworld? Notes on Habermas' Writings on Law'. Presented at Law & Society Association annual meeting, Philadelphia.

Raes, Koen (1986) 'Legislation, Communication and Strategy: A Critique of Habermas' Approach to Law', *Journal of Law and Society* 13: 183.

Robert, Philippe, ed. (1991), *La création de la loi et ses acteurs: L'exemple du droit pénal*. Oñati: IISJ (Oñati Proceedings 6).

Santos, Boaventura de Sousa (1985a) 'On Modes of Production of Law and Social Power', *International Journal of the Sociology of Law* 13: 299.

Santos, Boaventura de Sousa (1985b) 'Estado e Sociedade na Semiperiferia do Sistema Mundial: O caso português', *Análise Social* 21 (Lisbon, nos. 87/88/89): 869.

Santos, Boaventura de Sousa (1989) 'Towards a Post-Modern Understanding of Law', in André-Jean Arnaud (ed.) *Legal Culture and Everyday Life*, p. 113. Oñati: IISJ (Oñati Proceedings 1).

Santos, Boaventura de Sousa (1991) *State, Wage Relations and Social Welfare in the Semiperiphery: The Case of Portugal*. Coimbra: Oficina do CES, no. 23.

Savelsberg, Joachim S. (1987) 'The Making of Criminal Law Norms in Welfare States: Economic Crime in West Germany', *Law & Society Review* 21: 529.

Teubner, Gunther (1991) 'Autopoiesis and Steering: How Politics Profits from the Normative Surplus of Capital'. Presented at the joint meeting of the Law & Society Association and of the ISA Research Committee of Sociology of Law, Amsterdam.

Teubner, Gunther (1992) 'Regulatory Law: Chronicle of a Death Foretold', *Social & Legal Studies* 1: 451.

Trubek, David (1972) 'Max Weber on Law and the Rise of Capitalism', *Wisconsin Law Review* 720.

Tushnet, Mark (1988) 'Comment on Eder', *Law & Society Review* 22: 945 (see Eder, 1988).

Peter Bal

Discourse ethics and human rights in criminal procedure

Introduction

An important issue in contemporary societies is how to warrant the legitimacy of law. Legitimation of law calls for moral standards. Developments in modern law, however, show a disconnection from its traditional moral foundations and a tendency towards legal instrumentality in regulating highly complex societies. Focusing on the effectiveness of law and disregarding its normative premisses endangers the legitimacy of law.

That legitimate law is in need of moral standards is particularly vital for criminal law. In no other area of law do moral issues play such an important role.[1] Traditionally, many definitions of crime have been based on (common-sense) moral values.[2] Violating these values is considered such a serious offence that it is liable to criminal punishment. The governmental power to punish is most clearly expressed in imprisonment, not to mention the extreme possibility of capital punishment. As an intended infliction of pain, criminal punishment is the severest legal sanction we know. The foundations of criminal law concerning definitions of crime and the justification of punishment are of a predominantly moral nature.[3] The application of coercive means by law enforcement agencies raises moral issues as well in that criminal investigation usually involves a deprivation of liberty and an infringement of privacy and property.

Developments in the area of criminal law also indicate a detachment of its moral foundations. The emphasis nowadays lies on the effectiveness of criminal law in the struggle against crime. For this purpose it is expanding its scope and is mainly judged on its instrumental value as an effective crime-control policy. New criminalizations and harsher punishments are introduced as well as more far-reaching methods of criminal investigation. Even the legal protection of criminal suspects securing 'due process of law' threatens to be brought down. Rethinking the moral basis of both criminal law and proceedings, therefore, is a necessity to warrant their legitimacy.

Of the proposed solutions to the problem of the legitimacy of law, Habermas's theory of discourse ethics (1983, 1991 and 1992) seems very promising for a reappraisal of the moral basis of law. In this article I discuss Habermas's approach and examine the applicability of his theory to criminal law,[4] especially to criminal procedure.[5]

The first part deals with Habermas's view on opening legal procedures to a moral-practical discourse. I argue that his model of procedural rationality provides insufficient grounds for the legitimacy of law, because it includes only formal conditions for moral-legal argumentation without offering moral norms that can serve as substantive starting-points for this argumentation. To solve this problem of form and substance, a practical discourse in legal procedure must take some moral norms as its substantive point of departure. In this respect, I consider human rights to be the most likely candidates.

In the second part I show that the integration of a practical-legal discourse into criminal procedure is of special importance in creating a more symmetrical communication structure and expanding the scope of moral argumentation in forensic communication. I contend that human rights are the necessary substantive ingredients for this argumentation to guarantee the legitimacy of criminal law.

I Legal procedure and moral-practical discourse

1 Habermas versus Weber on legitimacy and the moral dimension of law

In any legal theory the relation between law and morality is problematic. Reflecting on this link is relevant to the issue of the legitimacy of law.

The 'classical' and still predominant view on the legitimacy of law is that of Weber (1956). His concept of formal rationality of law presupposes a strict separation of law from morality. According to Weber, law derives its legitimacy not from morality, but from its formal properties. These properties are:

1   a system of legal norms, developed by professional jurists, that
    bring order to existing social norms;
2   a legislature which creates laws that are generally valid and are
    formulated in the abstract; and
3   a judiciary and a government that are bound by these laws with
    regard to application and execution.

With these formal properties, law has a rationality of its own that is no
longer dependent on moral points of view.[6] Consequently, Weber
concluded that law and morality should be (and remain as) two
separated spheres. The legitimacy of law is, as he puts it, dependent not
on morality, but on legality.[7]

Habermas (1988) criticizes Weber's concept of formal rationality
of law. According to Habermas, law and morality are unbreakably
linked. The formal properties of law, as described by Weber, cannot be
seen as rational in a morally neutral sense and, therefore, cannot
guarantee the legitimacy of law. The legality of governmental power
exercised by means of positive law has no legitimate force of its own.
What is legal is not necessarily legitimate. Considering the formal
properties of law, Habermas argues that they have an implicit moral
dimension from which law derives its legitimacy. First, the systematiz-
ation of law by professional jurists contributes to legitimacy only when
it takes moral justifications into account. In positive law, social norms
have lost their validity based on custom. Because of this, legal norms
now need to be founded on moral principles. Second, general and
abstract laws are also dependent on moral principles for their
legitimate validity; for instance, treating equal cases as equal and
unequal as unequal. And third, the judiciary does not apply laws
blindly. In interpreting laws, moral views are involved. Decision-
making in concrete cases is not only a matter of black-letter law, but
(always) of normative considerations as well. Positive law should,
therefore, take this inherently moral dimension into account for its
legitimacy.

To ensure the legitimacy of law, Habermas states, legal procedures
(of law-making and application of law) must provide opportunities for
moral argumentation, i.e. a discussion about the rightness of normative validity claims. He considers the model of moral argumentation
in a practical discourse as an appropriate procedure for rational
decision-making. In such a procedure normative questions can be
judged from a moral point of view. In other words, legal discourse
must be perceived as a special kind of moral-practical discourse (Alexy,
1978).[8]

The conditions for a practical discourse are:

1   that it be free from coercion and power differences;
2   that it offer equal chances for participation;
3   that no topic shall be excluded from discussion; and
4   that the only accepted force shall be that of the better argument.

Under these conditions of an ideal speech-situation, participants will – in principle – be able to reach a rational consensus on moral issues.[9] In theory, at least, the outcome of such a discourse will be morally right and generally acceptable. This is, in short, the basic idea of discourse ethics according to which only those moral norms can claim to be universally valid that are agreed upon by all persons involved as participants in a practical discourse. The integration of a practical discourse into legal discourse will, therefore, contribute to the moral legitimacy of law.

My objection to Habermas's solution to the problem of the legitimacy of law is that his notion of procedural rationality does not prescribe any moral standards (Eder, 1986; 1988), but offers only a procedure with regard to the legitimacy of law. In other words, his view does not convey what kinds of moral norms are considered to be legitimate at the outset. Except for the principles of moral argumentation under strictly formal conditions of an ideal speech-situation, no generally acknowledged moral norms can be formulated. Consequently, the problem of legitimacy of law becomes a problem of form and substance.

2 The problem of form and substance

There has been discussion on the issue whether discursive ethics presupposes at least some moral norms or principles.

According to Honneth (1986), discourse ethics must go beyond the limits of moral formalism and include a substantive element – for instance, a concept of justice – in its normative presuppositions. This concept of justice not only implies that discourse ethics must offer participants an opportunity to engage equally in discourses, but also requires their capability to formulate moral standpoints.

In response to this kind of criticism, Habermas (1986b) stated that discourse ethics contains two substantive moral principles, i.e. justice and solidarity. Justice stands for equal respect and equal rights for all; solidarity for empathy and care for the well-being of our fellow human beings. Both these complementary principles correspond to the task morality must fulfil; on the one hand, ensuring the inviolability of individuals and their subjective dignity and, on the other hand, guaranteeing the intersubjective relations of mutual recognition between society's members.

With regard to the problem of form and substance, Honneth has postulated important substantive norms concerning the necessary conditions for realizing practical discourses. With the regulative principles justice and solidarity, Habermas has provided discourse ethics with a moral basis. Discourse ethics, therefore, is not entirely indifferent towards moral substance, nor towards the possibilities for its practical realization. These aspects are structurally embedded in the notion of discourse ethics. They remain, however, implicit and cannot be considered as moral norms that can readily produce arguments for the legitimacy of law. After all, only the outcome of discursive procedures will indicate what moral norms can claim to be generally valid. The only requirement is that, whatever these norms, they have to conduce towards justice and solidarity. The question can, therefore, be raised whether a procedural theory should not ultimately be based on substantive starting-points. For instance, should we not presuppose that discrimination on the basis of race or sex is immoral and, therefore, unjustifiable? Such moral standpoints need not be made dependent on the outcome of a practical discourse in order to be acknowledged as generally valid.

When the theory of discourse ethics wants to avoid moral indifference or neutrality, some explicit moral norms must be devised as the uncontested substance which will give a practical-legal discourse both content and further direction. In this respect, Dworkin's legal theory (1977; 1985; 1986) offers a possible solution to the problem of form and substance with regard to the legitimacy of law. He criticizes procedural theories on democracy, law and morality that disregard fundamental arguments (Ely, 1980). Law cannot be applied and interpreted without using substantive, normative arguments. Legal reasoning is based on fundamental moral principles that are embodied in constitutional rights. These rights offer citizens protection against their fellow citizens and against the government. They cannot simply be ignored by majority opinions or by the general interest. In that sense they are important instruments for the legal protection of minorities and, therefore, should be taken seriously. Constitutional rights contain both moral and civil-political rights. Thus, this view implies that the judge can no longer be considered an impartial figure. In interpreting constitutional rights, it is necessary that judges take a moral and political stand. These rights are the starting-points for judicial decision-making.

Although Dworkin explicitly refers to substantive moral principles as they are incorporated in American constitutional rights, his solution to the problem of the legitimacy of law is still insufficient. In order for rights to be considered as substantive moral guidelines for legitimate decision-making, they must be universally valid and not be 'limited' to American constitutional rights. In other words, their validity must be generally acknowledged and agreed upon by participants in rational discourse. The question is, therefore, what rights can claim such discursively founded validity?

3 Human rights as the moral substance of practical-legal discourse

Habermas (1985) argued that morality is universal, 'if it permits only norms of which all those concerned could approve on the basis of full consideration and without duress. No one will object to that – the basic rights and the principles of our constitutions are norms which we may assume everyone could affirm' (p. 90). Their validity knows no limits and, according to Habermas, 'even subjects political action to moral scrutiny' (p. 91). Thus, he also appeals to constitutional rights (in case of both the United States and 'Western' Germany) which he assumes already contain universal moral norms that will hold up in rational discourse. In fact, he anticipates a likely outcome of such a discourse. But, how can these rights be connected with the problem of legitimacy?

In his latest work on the discourse theory of law Habermas (1992) states that the legitimacy of (positive) law is dependent on the acknowledgement of a system of fundamental rights. These rights contain the right to equal subjective liberties or freedom of action guaranteeing private autonomy and the right to equal participation in the democratic will-formation process warranting political autonomy. With regard to the right to equal liberties (and its correlated rights to civil membership of a voluntary association of legal subjects and to legal protection in exercising one's rights), Habermas asserts that no legitimate law can exist without such rights (p. 159). He considers these (subjective) rights as fundamental legal principles ('Rechtsprinzipien') that must be specified by the political legislature. Therefore, they do not (yet) embody the classical, liberal constitutional rights, like those to human dignity, to life, personal freedom and physical inviolability, to property, etc. The latter rights are interpretations and elaborations of the general right to equal liberties by the legislature.[10]

With these legal principles, Habermas has provided the foundations for the legitimacy of law.[11] Since the legislature has formulated constitutional rights in accordance with these principles, it can – in my view – be argued that precisely these rights are legitimate. They incorporate moral norms everyone could affirm.

Taking this one step further, it can be asserted that this also counts for human rights as framed in international declarations and conventions.[12] Most constitutional rights have merged into the broader framework of human rights. They claim universal validity and there is a growing worldwide consensus on this point. Human rights can be considered the moral core of law.[13] The theory of discourse ethics could take these rights as a substantive point of departure.[14] In other words, moral argumentation in law could be guided by the 'moral demands of human rights' (Campbell, 1986).

As a consequence of taking human rights as the starting-points for a practical-legal discourse, the moral standard for the legitimacy of law is to be found not only in the formal conditions of a practical-legal discourse, but also in the minimal moral substance of human rights.

Does this mean that human rights automatically precede practical discourses and, therefore, are beyond dispute? This would contradict the claim that a practical discourse is the last instance with regard to normative questions and that no topic may be excluded from discussion.

Chambers (1992) states that constitutional rights do not have precedence over discourses, for we cannot appreciate their value without a discourse. Since practical discourses are necessarily embedded in the lifeworld from which they obtain their themes of discussion, they incorporate what we already commonly share, like constitutional rights. These rights, such as, for example, freedom of expression, are an important part of our tradition. According to Chambers the discursive problematization of these rights poses no threat to their (general) validity as such. On the contrary, in a practical discourse these rights (and their supporting consensus) can be strengthened. There is no need to fear that they will be discarded in a practical discourse. In fact, some rights, such as those to personal freedom, to equal treatment and to mutual respect, belong to the enabling conditions for practical discourses. The question whether rights have precedence over discourses is, therefore, rather pointless. They presuppose each other. Rights always need to be demanded, justified and founded in argumentation processes. Disconnected from discourses they are incomplete. Even when rights have found a strong footing, they will not fall beyond the discursive scope, but can, in the background of discourses, foster our arguments.

Chambers's analysis concerning constitutional rights also applies to human rights. On the basis of these considerations, I conclude that human rights can be taken as minimal substantive moral guidelines of practical-legal discourses and that from them we can derive arguments for the legitimacy of law.

In the next part, I deal with the question whether this theoretical approach of discourse ethics and human rights applies to the domain of criminal law. First, I examine what a discursive arrangement of criminal procedure means for the scope of moral-legal argumentation. Second, I address the issue of the implementation of procedural rationality in the criminal justice system. Finally, I discuss how human rights can provide moral standards for the legitimacy of criminal law.

II Practical-legal discourse in criminal procedure

1 Widening and deepening of forensic communication in criminal cases

If legal procedures should give room to a practical discourse, so should criminal procedure, all the more since the link between law and morality is particularly vital for criminal law.

First, I discuss how Habermas (1992) applies discourse ethics to legal procedures in general. Second, I argue that his application is rather limited, especially with regard to criminal procedure. And third, I present my view on a discursive arrangement of criminal procedure.

Application of discourse ethics to legal procedures. Habermas addresses the following issues:

1   the relation between a practical and a legal discourse;
2   the conditions for a practical-legal discourse and their implementation; and
3   the opportunities they provide for (factual and) moral argumentation.

(1) Habermas points out that (any) forensic communication necessarily takes place under restrictions which impede its measuring up to the standard of rational discourse. The most problematic impediment is that a legal discourse – unlike a practical discourse – cannot guarantee the (one and only) right decision. A practical discourse is directed towards the establishment of the (universal) rightness of normative validity claims ('Geltungsdiskurs'). According to Habermas (1992), following Günther (1989) on this point, a legal discourse is, therefore, not fully compatible with a practical discourse. A legal discourse is, after all, not aimed at testing the validity of legal norms, but rather at the most appropriate ('angemessen') application of a set of prima-facie valid norms to a specific situation ('Anwendungs-diskurs'). A full description of all relevant features of that situation

must determine which norms collide with regard to their applicability to the case in hand. On the basis of this description, the argumentation process will impartially establish which norm has preference above the other(s) and can be appropriately applied to the situation. This argumentation process allows the yielding norms to preserve their general (prima-facie) validity. A legal discourse must, in other words, be relieved from questions of validity and be directed towards questions of application only. At most, it can warrant an appropriate decision, given the rightness of the presupposed validity of legal norms set by the legislature. We must keep in mind that the legitimacy of legal norms is ultimately based on the reasonableness ('Vernünftigkeit') of the democratic process of political lawmaking.[15] However, there are strong reasons to believe that this is not always the case. Both the (legal) procedures of lawmaking and the procedures of application of law must deal with a deficiency by acknowledging that the ideal conditions of rational discourse can only be approximately realized. How can this be done?

(2) According to Habermas, legal procedural rules (for the application of law) must shape an institutional framework securing 'open' forensic communication under (external) temporal, social and pragmatic conditions, without interfering with the (inner) logic of argumentation as such.

Habermas uses civil and criminal procedures as examples to show how these conditions are implemented. First, temporal conditions guarantee that procedures come to a close within a reasonable amount of time. Second, the division of social roles warrants the symmetry between the conflicting parties, plaintiff and defendant. And third, pragmatic conditions assure that the topic of legal dispute is clearly defined (beforehand) with regard to the facts and juridical merits of the case.

But, is there room for legal discourse within this framework?

(3) Habermas states that the process of presenting factual evidence in court is not structured discursively per se.[16] The parties in conflict are not obliged to cooperate in truth-finding. In fact, they usually try, by strategic interaction, to reach a favourable outcome which reflects their best interests. This is why truth-finding is not necessarily a cooperative but rather a competitive enterprise. Still, it offers enough room for all relevant facts to be broached. Eventually, it is the perspective of the judge that is the constitutive factor for an impartial 'objective' determination of truth.

When it comes to the juridical interpretation and appreciation of these facts, Habermas asserts that this is the 'real' legal discourse. This is where moral arguments come into play. It is, however, (only) the judge who assesses the considered true facts according to his professional knowledge. The verdict he renders in public contains the grounds that support his decision. The legal remedy system provides a further guarantee that a legal discourse can be continued in appeal, so that other judges can put the verdict to the test.

Limitations in application. In my opinion Habermas's application of his theory to criminal procedure is rather 'limited'.

(1) I agree that a legal discourse in criminal procedure is primarily a discourse of application and, therefore, not fully compatible with a practical discourse, only so far as this does not preclude room for moral argumentation. The question is whether this moral argumentation should be limited only to an interpretation of presumedly valid norms regarding their applicability, and thereby reducing the possibility of problematizing their prima-facie validity. This is dependent on what norms are to be considered indisputably valid from the outset and form a coherent system of norms. As I have argued, this claim can be attributed to human rights. However, it cannot be asserted of all criminal legal norms that possibly apply to specific cases. For instance, just as I might expect the judiciary to be reluctant in applying the prohibitive norm of unlawful coercion in response to a sit-in demonstration,[17] I can imagine it questioning the validity of a law criminalizing all kinds of preparatory activities,[18] since this may lead to a criminal law of bad conscience ('Gesinnungsstrafrecht').

Viewing the deficiency of the democratic lawmaking process as a compromise formation where both moral and especially goal-oriented arguments are deciding factors, an argument can be made in favour of opening moral discourse in criminal procedure to question the presupposed legitimacy of legal norms. Developments in criminal procedural law, for instance, indicate a 'simplification' of formal rules that must prevent defendants' profiting from 'mere technicalities' and an expansion of coercive investigative means (telephone-tapping, shadowing, undercover activities, etc.). These developments undermine the legal position and protection of defendants and are explicitly intended to get a more effective grasp on crime. The extension of the scope of criminal law by new criminalizations of, for instance, preparatory actions, conspiracy and computer 'hacking' is also prompted by demands of an effective crime-control policy. In this respect, it is necessary to review the moral foundations of criminal law to critically assess these changes on their legitimacy. I consider this a special task and responsibility of both the judiciary and criminal defence.

(2) With regard to the social condition of forensic communication, the symmetrical role-division might generally be true for civil

procedure. However, in continental criminal procedure the likeliness of equal communication still leaves much to be desired. The asymmetrical distribution of speaking roles rather restrains forensic communication. The course of courtroom interaction can even be considered coercive communication.[19] The judge is leading the interrogation and generally directs the verbal interaction to a confirmation of the charges through the use of suggestive and – sometimes even – insinuating questions and of 'indisputable' assertions from the police records. The defendant is forced to comply with both factual and normative presuppositions underlying the speech-acts of the judge that afford him or her hardly any opportunity to give an own view of the situation. There is no 'authority' that can exercise communicative control over the judge's verbal performance in court, as an Anglo-American 'passive' judge can do to the cross-examining parties. Therefore, it can be said that the asymmetrical role-division does interfere with the (inner) logic of argumentation in that certainly not all aspects of the legal conflict are openly debatable. Moreover, the pragmatic condition imposes restraints on forensic communication, since the indictment is already formulated in strictly juridical terms in which framework 'reality' has to be reconstructed. This reconstruction of reality in court does not allow for another – particularly the defendant's – version of the situation.

(3) Under these conditions there seems little opportunity for a practical-legal discourse. Regarding a practical-legal discourse in criminal cases, Habermas leaves this almost completely up to the judiciary. Although I agree that it is finally from this perspective that a decision on both factual and moral matters must be reached, I am troubled by the fact that participants only contribute to the process of truth-finding in a strategic way, while being excluded from moral reasoning regarding the facts. And, as far as this is left solely to the judiciary it remains, as Habermas states, 'unthematic in the background' (p. 289), despite the fact that – as he indicates – factual and legal-moral questions are necessarily interrelated. Because of the presumed separation between matters of fact and of legal appreciation, the interaction of the parties is limited to the determination of facts and assurance of proof. Accordingly, it is my opinion that a legal discourse becomes a monological rather than dialogical enterprise. In fact, only in appeal cases does the judiciary communicate the moral-legal issues, albeit not directly (i.e. in a vertical, hierarchical line) and mainly on paper (i.e. the parties are not always present).[20] Habermas's own application of discourse ethics to criminal procedure, therefore, only gives the parties in conflict an 'equal' opportunity to participate in a 'theoretical' discourse on the facts where strategic interaction seems to be preponderant.

Discursive arrangement of criminal procedure. In my opinion, such an arrangement should provide ample opportunity for a critical and fundamental discussion.

In criminal procedure the topics of discussion are not only of a moral character, but also of a factual and psychological nature. Therefore, the other types of discourse that Habermas discerns[21] are also applicable.

In continental[22] criminal procedure, four basic questions are posed in which different validity claims are raised:

1 Has the defendant committed the (f)act as charged?
2 Is this act a punishable act according to criminal law?
3 Is the defendant guilty of this punishable act?

When these questions are answered affirmatively, a final question needs to be asked:

4 What sort of punishment can and must be imposed on the defendant?

The core themes of these questions concern the determination of: (a) the 'true' facts of the defendant's action, (b) the unlawfulness or moral wrongfulness of the defendant's action, (c) the defendant's personal accountability for the action, and (d) the most suitable penal reaction.

According to the conditions of argumentation in discourses, all participants equally contribute to the above-mentioned determinations. These determinations involve validity claims of (objective) truth, (intersubjective) rightness and (subjective) sincerity.[23]

The predominant goal of (contemporary) criminal procedure is truth-finding. Thus, the emphasis seems to lie on a 'theoretical' discourse to establish what 'really' happened. The other questions deal more with normative issues. This means that the moral recognition of allegedly violated legal norms, the moral wrongfulness of the violation, the personal accountability for the violation, and the justification of the sanction to be imposed, can all be made a topic of practical discourse. In fact, inasmuch as criminal procedure allows for moral argumentation, this type of argumentation will be predominant.[24]

This has far-reaching consequences for both criminal law and procedure. The presumed consensus of criminal law as a moral code of fixed conceptions of crime, of guilt, and of punishment, can be challenged in criminal procedure. As a result, criminal procedure is more independent of substantive or 'material' criminal law. The institutionalization of criminal procedure as a practical-legal discourse would signify that this procedure can no longer be considered as a simple means of realizing or applying substantive criminal law. The process of argumentation is, after all, directed at reaching a consensus whereby participants can speak freely about challenged validity claims of moral rightness. There are no limitations on themes and contributions. In principle, every participant can raise any topic and can refute or sustain any (factual and) normative assertion with the force of the better argument. Not only can the presupposed legitimacy of legal norms be questioned, but also – accepting their validity – the moral wrongfulness of the punishable act in question (by means of justifications), the individual responsibility for the act (by means of excuses), and desirability and acceptability of a (punitive) sanction, are worthy of moral reasoning. In theory, therefore, a practical-legal discourse in criminal procedure opens up possibilities of widening and deepening the discussions about moral issues in criminal law. A necessary condition, however, is that it provide sufficient room for open and unrestrained forensic communication.

I have argued that a discursive arrangement of criminal procedure can lay a foundation for truly moral-legal argumentation. In my opinion, this view is not far removed from that of Habermas, although he himself does not dilate upon criminal law. He refers to Günther (1991), who examined the role of discourse ethics for the foundation of criminal law. According to the central principle of discourse ethics, a norm claims universal validity only when the consequences and side-effects of a general compliance with this norm for the interests of every subject can be accepted by all. This means that every subject must be able to take the perspective of every other subject in judging the validity of a norm. This universal role-exchange guarantees that everyone's interest is weighed. The willingness to accept an intersubjective exchange of roles and perspectives belongs to the very conditions we must all fulfil as participants in rational argumentation. From this fundamental principle, Günther infers that the basic task of criminal law is to protect the elementary aspects of everyone's role as participant in interactions. With regard to the foundation of criminal law, he suggests that we should take a step beyond current ethics and theories of 'legal goods' ('Rechtsgüter') which serve as its basis of legitimacy. Criminal law should secure the conditions under which we can come to a normative consensus. This implies that the rightness of validity claims for current 'moral' or 'goods-oriented' foundations of criminal law must be suspended. Which moral norms need to be protected by criminal law and in what way this should be done, is a matter of lawmaking and application of law. For this purpose these practices must be structured discursively. Günther's discursive foundation of criminal law offers possibilities to widen and deepen criminal discourse along the lines I indicated above. Following Strawson's analysis of moral feelings, Günther convincingly demonstrates how, for instance, the questions of morally harmful behaviour and moral accountability can be reconsidered discursively. When it comes to morally blaming the offender we may not leave the participation perspective and take an 'objective' observational stance towards him. In other words, we must maintain communication with the offender. Only when all the perspectives (of victim, offender and society) are openly discussed, can the moral wrongfulness of an inflicted injury or insult be assessed. Moreover, this open discussion allows the offender to accept his or her moral liability.

In my view, Günther gives only an argument for a discursive restructuring of criminal law and procedure, without offering substantive moral norms that deserve legal protection (through criminal law) and that can serve as guidelines for forensic communication (in discussing the moral issues). In this respect, he remains faithful to the formal character of discourse ethics. But, since it can be said that the task of criminal law, protecting participatory roles in rational argumentation, counts for all law in general, he fails to be more specific. The most distinctive feature of criminal law is that, unlike any other area of law, it is so closely tied to moral issues. Thus, I think it is necessary to specify moral norms that could form the basis for a legitimate deployment of criminal law; norms that could lay foundations for criminal lawmaking and the administration of criminal justice. For this purpose human rights must be considered. As I have indicated, they can serve as basic moral standards in legal discourse. I will argue that they are particularly relevant for guiding moral argumentation in criminal discourse. Before going into this, I examine the implementation of procedural rationality in the contemporary criminal law system.

2 Proceduralization of criminal justice

Does a practical discourse fit into criminal procedure?

According to de Haan (1990), a practical discourse is not compatible with and not integratable into criminal procedure. He claims that criminal law 'has been a form of organized state power from its inception. Criminal justice must, therefore, be seen as a medium of power – the power to punish – rather than an institution for resolving moral conflicts' (p. 163). Definitions of crime and the justification of punishment cannot be challenged in criminal procedure. Criminal procedure is only a means of realizing the goals of criminal law: crime control. He refers to Habermas's analysis of developments in modern law (1981), according to which law has become a medium for systemic integration rather than an institution for normative integration. As a medium, law is considered a means of realizing goal-oriented action that has replaced or 'colonized' law as an institution. As an institution, law is connected with the lifeworld and the moral beliefs that exist therein.[25] This development also took place in the criminal law area. Criminal law has been disconnected from morality and separated from the lifeworld and has become a systemic instrument for effective crime control (Peters, 1986). Accordingly, the emphasis of criminal procedure is on effectiveness in the struggle against crime. Thus, a practical discourse in criminal procedure can only contribute to the legitimation of the instrumental character of the criminal justice system.[26]

De Haan's solution is to reconceptualize crime and punishment in terms of the lifeworld and reallocate practices involved in crime control into the matrix of social relations. In short, he proposes a differentiated 'politics of redress'. Here, the model of a practical discourse is of great importance, but not within the margins of criminal justice. This view emanates from the ideas of penal abolitionism. It implies that criminal law and procedure should dissolve and that the forms of conflict resolution which were once governmentally controlled should instead be shaped by citizens, who would actively participate. In these practices of 'informal or popular justice' the parties that are involved in a conflict define this conflict themselves with regard to the injuries suffered and damages done (instead of being bound by definitions of crime and subjected to criminal proceedings). They try – through a process of negotiation – to reach a settlement resulting in 'redress' (instead of criminal punishment). What crime is, is no longer fixed in advance. Moreover, the arsenal of 'sanctions' and their justifications are no longer uncontested concepts. Procedures of conflict resolution shaped after the model of a practical discourse must be embedded in the lifeworld, where they belong. According to de Haan, however, procedures of conflict resolution require legality and, therefore, remain dependent on rules and principles ensuring 'legal' security and equality. As a result, 'necessary' law is strictly of a formal nature.

This brings me back to the concept of legal procedures securing generally acknowledged decisions. After all, a discursive theory of law makes the acceptability of judicial decisions dependent on the structure of the argumentation process. It is this notion of procedural rationality that guarantees legal equality and security by a discursive deliberation on factual and moral-legal questions. But, what makes a legal procedure preferable to a practical discourse?

Habermas (1988) emphasized that legal procedures have advantages over practical discourses in the lifeworld. A practical discourse cannot guarantee infallibility, unambiguity, or the establishment of a result within a limited period of time. In principle, it is an open-ended project. Besides this cognitive shortcoming, a practical discourse suffers from a motivational weakness. To reach the 'right' moral decision, participants have to dissociate themselves from their 'taken-for-granted' lifeworld. This newly gained moral insight will, therefore, be quite remote from their everyday 'moral' way of life. There is no assurance that this insight gives a motivational force to act accordingly. Therefore, the procedural rationality of a practical discourse is incomplete. The more morality is internalized and becomes autonomous, the more it withdraws to the private realm. That is why social problems that ask for a unequivocal and binding regulation cannot be solved by leaving them to practical-moral reasoning. Instead, legal norms (set by the legislature) and procedures (of application) have to offer an imperative compensation for the uncertainties of pure morally guided human action. Morality as a system of cultural knowledge ('Wissenssystem') must be supplemented by compulsory law. Law is both a system of knowledge and of action ('Handlungssystem') (Habermas, 1992).

As indicated above, legal procedures are formalized in the sense that external and internal restrictions are neutralized to ensure the conditions of an ideal speech-situation as much as possible. They contain rules for the opening and the ending of discussions, for the topics of discussion, for the sequences of turn-taking, etc. Another important feature of legal procedures is the real and immediate pressure to reach binding decisions within a reasonable amount of time. Although legal procedures, especially criminal procedures, still leave much to be desired with regard to the conditions of an ideal speech-situation, they come closer to the demands of procedural rationality. Contrary to practical discourses in the lifeworld, a legal procedure can underpin its outcome by (the threat and imposition of) sanctions commanding observance to the final result. This is because in positive law, legally institutionalized expectations of behaviour obtain a binding force by relating them to the state arsenal of sanctions that can be imposed when these expectations are violated. As I have argued, a discursive arrangement of criminal procedure provides ample opportunities for a critical and fundamental discussion. In such a discussion no topic is beyond dispute. The legal concepts of crime and criminal punishment, therefore, always remain debatable. This is, however, only possible inasmuch as criminal procedure increases its autonomous significance and obtains an independent position in discussing matters of criminal justice.

What are the 'actual' possibilities of implementing procedural rationality in criminal procedure? Contrary to what de Haan (1990) assumes, the prospects of this are rather favourable for the following reasons.

1   Judge-made law has become more important for legal develop-ment. A strict separation of legislative, executive and judiciary powers no longer exists. As a matter of fact, in many legal systems a proceduralization process has taken place. The judiciary construes the rules of substantive criminal law and formal procedural law. Matters of substantive criminal law are now more frequently being dealt with in criminal procedure.[27] This is especially the case when judicial decisions have to be taken under rapidly changing social circumstances and where a change of law by the legislature cannot be awaited (i.e. in cases of euthanasia[28] and abortion). This judicial 'activism', however, is still bound by (the presupposed legitimate validity of) legal norms set by the legislature in democratic procedures. Nonetheless, it has resulted in a more independent attitude towards positive law.

2   In addition, judicial review of the constitutionality of laws is now widely accepted.[29] Under judicial review, the legitimate validity of laws can be measured against the constitution. Constitutional rights and above all, as I have argued, human rights, form a last resort for testing the validity of legal norms as they are incorpor-ated in laws. Habermas (1992) also assumes that judicial review is ultimately 'limited' to an application of the norms embedded in the constitution. The validity of these norms has to be presupposed. In fact, they contain the principles for a constructive interpretation (Dworkin's term) by the judiciary. This opens possibilities to assess the legitimacy of positive law from a moral point of view.

In the final section I argue that procedural rationality is, to some extent, already formally guaranteed in the provisions of human rights conventions which detail the directives for legal procedures, especially criminal procedure. Within the framework of these formal require-ments human rights must also provide the substantive moral guidelines for practical-legal discourse.

3 Instrumentalization versus constitutionalization of criminal justice

Criminal procedure – both in continental and Anglo-American legal systems – has been subjected to principles that have to secure a fair administration of justice. These principles are intended to strengthen the legal protection of defendants. Such protection places restrictions on the far-reaching coercive means used by governmental agencies to 'find the truth'. The procedural principles are incorporated in constitutional and human rights. The relevance of these rights for criminal justice is evident, for there is no social institution in which these rights are so much at stake (Hassemer, 1988). The functioning of criminal justice is attended by an infringement of these rights. That is why constitutions and human rights conventions contain special procedural norms to secure 'due process of law' and 'equality of arms'. These norms, however, are of a predominantly formal nature. They provide conditions for a 'fair trial' and are aimed at offering the defendant an equal chance of participation.

These procedural norms are conceived as a counterbalance to instrumental criminal policies that are mainly directed at the repression of crime. Still the 'old' controversy between 'crime control' and 'due process' (Packer, 1968), or instrumentality versus legal protection, has not ended. Looking at recent developments in criminal procedure, there are tendencies towards a more instrumental criminal policy curtailing defendants' rights. Indications for this restriction can be found in American Federal Supreme Court decisions over the past decades.[30] Comparatively, in continental criminal law systems the legal protection of defendants also came heavily under pressure. In this respect, it is interesting to see what the European Court of Human Rights has done[31] and will do with regard to possible (national) violations of procedural human rights as laid down in the European Convention on Human Rights. When criminal lawyers focus on human rights, they mainly refer to the specific procedural rights. Since these formal rights are considered fundamental, the (ongoing) instrumentalization of criminal justice should ultimately find its limit in these rights. They should be taken 'seriously' and be preserved at all costs.

However, human rights should play another, more substantive, role in criminal procedure. As indicated, moral issues can be fully discussed in a practical-legal discourse. The possible topics of discussion are the moral bond of legal norms, the moral wrongfulness of an alleged violation of these norms, the accountability for this violation and the moral justification of the punishment. I will demonstrate how human rights could be taken as moral guidelines for a substantive discussion on these topics.

The first – and most basic – issue concerns the acknowledgement of norms that should be protected by criminal law. If we consider human rights as a moral point of reference, they should form the basis for criminalization and decriminalization processes.[32] Definitions of crime have to be founded on serious violations of fundamental human rights. In this view, the social harm or impropriety of human actions is dependent on the way in which and the extent to which these actions affect basic human values (Hassemer, 1991). This could legitimize their protection through criminal law. By rethinking the moral basis of criminal law from a human rights perspective, criminalizations (and the penalties involved) can be reduced to a hard core of forms of injustice that threaten generalizable interests. As a result, it will be possible to be 'frugal' with criminal law. It would clearly demonstrate that many social problems cannot be solved by criminal law, but that other areas of law (like civil or administrative law, which have less severe sanctions at their disposal), or even non-legal means offer more appropriate solutions.

The role that human rights could play in propositions for decriminalization can be illustrated by parallel analysis of how (national) constitutional rights can be related to, for instance, the problem of drugs. According to Bollinger (1992), the (German) criminalization of any kind of drug use can be considered as a violation of constitutional rights. Taking the constitutional right to personal freedom as a starting-point, a procedure for criminalization must fulfil two conditions: first, a fundamental right must have been violated causing substantial social harm; and, second, criminalization is the proper response to avoid this harm. The anti-drug laws are contrary to these conditions, because drug use does not cause serious social harm and – as can be empirically documented – criminal law is not a suitable instrument to 'tackle' this problem. His most important argument is that drug use is an expression of constitutional rights itself and that accordingly, criminalization violates these rights. He refers to such rights as the right to personal privacy, allowing freedom of and respect for diverse life-styles in a multicultural society, among which is included the use of drugs; the right to self-determination and personal inviolability, permitting you to bring harm to yourself; and the right to equal treatment, implying that drug use should not be dealt with any differently from other stimulants such as smoking cigarettes or drinking alcohol. Putting aside the question whether his arguments are sound in every respect, this attempt to review the constitutionality of criminal policy is an interesting line of approach.[33] From this perspective it can, for instance, be argued that the problem of drug use can better be handled by public health services than by criminal law.

Within the margins of prohibitive norms, constitutional and human rights are also vital in discussing the issue of moral wrongful-ness of an alleged violation of these norms. Such a violation can be justified if committed under specific circumstances. A justification – provided that it has been accepted – 'takes away' the punishability or moral wrongfulness of an otherwise penal act. In discussions on the plausibility and acceptability of justifications, fundamental rights are involved, as can be shown by criminal-legal disputes on the punishability of, for instance, certain practices of euthanasia and abortion. In these cases different rights collide with regard to their preference, like those to life (and its protection) and to self-determination. In defining the boundaries between punishable and non-punishable forms of euthanasia and abortion, the legislature and the judiciary must necessarily engage in moral argumentation about the invoked rights and strike a careful balance between them.[34] Legalization of abortion and euthanasia cannot provide a licence to do as one likes, but should define clear conditions under which these practices can go unpunished or will not be prosecuted. These justifying exceptions of punishability or of prosecutability cannot be determined only by, for instance, the medical profession or the people most concerned. In any form, legislative and/or judicial control remain(s) necessary because fundamental human rights and interests are at stake. In this respect, both criminal law and procedure perform the roles of moral guardians in these matters, but should allow the debate to remain open.

Moreover, in criminal cases human rights and their social, economical and cultural counterparts[35] could be relevant with regard to the problem of accountability. The latter rights demand from a government an active policy to realize equal opportunities for its citizens exercising their individual rights. They include rights to labour, social security, education, public health and cultural identity and diversity. When governments fail to realize these rights, this failure can be considered a causative factor of crime. By referring to forms of 'social injustice' the judiciary could hold this against society;[36] however, not in a deterministic way by taking away someone's individual responsibility.[37] Still, it can contribute to a better understanding of the causes of various kinds of crime that should be reckoned with in criminal procedure. Moral liability is not only a subjective matter, but also a social, economical and cultural concern.

Finally, human rights could play a substantive part in the justification and execution of criminal punishment. It is, therefore, necessary to determine what sort of human rights violation justifies imprisonment. Human rights proponents would argue that the deprivation of liberty should be restricted to an *ultimum remedium*, not to mention that capital punishment is completely unjustifiable. Assuming a deprivation of liberty is justified as a sanction to the violation of moral norms, this deprivation should not go any further than the necessary isolation from society. This means that other fundamental rights should remain unimpeded, like the right to family life, labour, education, property, free expression and gathering, etc.

Thus, the conditions of imprisonment also must be reviewed by human rights.[38]

By taking human rights 'seriously' in substantive debates on criminal law matters, a moral counterbalance can be afforded to predominantly instrumental criminal policies. The answers to practically all questions in both criminal law and procedure concerning (de)criminalization of human action, social and individual responsibility, necessity of punishment, priorities in law enforcement and treatment of suspects, defendants and inmates, require moral arguments that can be derived from human rights. They can lay the ultimate foundation for the credibility and legitimacy of criminal justice.

Rijksuniversiteit Limburg, the Netherlands

Notes

I wish to thank Willem de Haan, Mathieu Deflem and Whitney Bell for their critical comments on an earlier draft.

1   This view is also held by Habermas (1992). In an 'excursion' on the moral content of law (p. 251), he states that the weight of this content is dependent on reactions to norm violations, i.e. the moral indignation and the imposed sanctions. In this respect civil and criminal law differ significantly.

2   From a liberal perspective, however, criminal law should not enforce moral values. 'What is proposed is a restricted and morally neutral definition of harm, a commitment of legal agencies to preventing harms of the relevant kinds, and beyond that a refusal to establish any particular set of moral (or religious) values in the norms of the criminal law' (MacCormick, 1991: 221). The extensive growth of regulatory criminal law in western societies is an indication of moral disestablishment of crime definitions. However, it cannot be denied that whatever concepts of social harm or protectable goods ('Rechtsgüter') one adheres to, they necessarily imply some kind of moral choice.

3   Also MacCormick (1991: 222): '(t)he concept, the apparatus and the practice of punishment are, and are necessarily (in my view), significantly moralistic in content for otherwise punishments could not have the symbolic, communicative and expressive functions which are essential to the practice.'

4   In the introduction to his latest work, Habermas (1992) explicitly refrains from entering the discussion on the foundations of criminal law (p. 9). For an application of discourse ethics to this area he refers to the contribution of Günther (1991). His approach will also be further discussed below.

5   In this article I mainly refer to continental (Dutch) criminal law. Criminal law is the overall term for the domain of law that consists of substantive (material) and formal (procedural) criminal law. Substantive criminal law contains the definitions of penalized acts, the conditions of punishability and the maximum penalties that can be imposed. Formal criminal law includes the rules (and principles) for the administration of criminal justice. These rules regulate criminal procedure in realizing substantive criminal law through the diverse stages of investigation, prosecution, adjudication and sentencing. Although the trial is only a small part of criminal procedure, this is the stage where a definite decision is made whether the defendant committed a criminal act for which he or she can be held liable and be sentenced. When I speak of criminal procedure, I refer to this stage. Despite structural differences between common and state criminal law, it is my contention that the discourse theory applies to both legal systems. The 'adversarial' and 'inquisitorial' systems of criminal procedure differ mostly with regard to courtroom interaction. In an adversarial system, the parties more autonomously search for truth by means of cross-examination in front of a 'passive' judge, while in an inquisitorial system the judge is actively searching for truth by leading the conversation and interrogation. It can, therefore, be said that the communication structure in an Anglo-American criminal court is more equal than in a continental one. Another major difference is that common criminal law is mainly judge-made law. There is no (one and only) code of substantive criminal law, nor a code of procedural law. In state law, it is the substantive criminal law that has to be applied by the judiciary according to procedural law. When it comes to systematic comparisons between the two systems, it appears that there are more similarities than differences. On the one hand, substantive criminal law becomes more important in the United States of America by the introduction of the 'Model Penal Code', while on the continent judge-made law becomes more prominent. On the other hand, the pre-trial stages of criminal procedure show similarities with regard to the coercive methods used by investigating and prosecuting agencies. They are both governed by constitutional rules and principles that have to secure 'due process of law' and offer the defendant the necessary legal protection.

6   The legality of governmental power can claim to be legitimate as far as

law-making is strictly bound by formal procedures in setting the rules ('Satzungsprinzip'). This formal rationality of law implies that law is value-neutral and no longer dependent on a moral (material) justification ('Begründungsprinzip'). According to Weber moral views are only subjective value-orientations whose content cannot be rationalized and are, therefore, incompatible with the formal character of law. After all, a formal and rational legal system provides general norms that are binding for all citizens and independent from personal values.

7   This view is still held and further elaborated by, for instance, Luhmann (1983).

8   Following Günther (1989) in his critique on Alexy (1978), Habermas (1992) now states that a legal discourse is not a special kind ('Sonderfall') of a practical discourse, but a moral discourse of application ('Anwendungsdiskurs'). I discuss this view in further detail in the text.

9   In his earlier work, Habermas (1981) distinguished a theoretical discourse and aesthetic/therapeutic critique from a practical discourse. The focus of discussion here is respectively on testing the validity claims of truth, sincerity and rightness. As Habermas has indicated, these validity claims are simultaneously put forward by speakers in their speech-acts in everyday communicative interactions. These validity claims correspond to the verbal representation of objective facts, the disclosure of speakers' subjectivity, and the establishment of legitimate social relations or norms. In everyday conversations we usually take for granted or tacitly assume that the validity claims are fulfilled, i.e. that we speak the truth ('Wahrheit'), are sincere in our utterances ('Wahrhaftigkeit') and are convinced of the rightness of the norms that regulate our interactions ('Richtigkeit'). However, when doubts are raised or conflicts arise about this, we enter into a discourse putting the problematized validity claim to the test. On the basis of argumentative grounds (under the conditions of an ideal speech-situation) we try to reach a consensus on this claim. In each of the above-mentioned types of discourse one of those validity claims is the central topic of discussion.

10 The correlated rights to civil membership of a voluntary association of legal subjects and to legal protection in exercising one's rights are respectively specified in, for instance, injunction of extradition, right of asylum, 'non bis in idem' and equal access to an impartial tribunal (p. 159).

11 Although Habermas states that the legitimacy of law is dependent on the acknowledgement of these legal principles, he still holds that the legitimacy of law is ultimately ('letztlich') dependent on a

communicative arrangement, i.e. on democratic procedures (p. 134). Thus, he seems to give priority to discourses above rights.

12 When Habermas (1992) speaks of human rights ('Menschenrechte'), he refers to the unspecified subjective rights. In my terminology human rights stand for the rights that are specified in the Universal Declaration of Human Rights (Paris 1948), the European Convention on the Protection of Human Rights and Fundamental Freedoms (Rome 1950) and the International Treaty on Civil and Political Rights (New York 1966), and the correlated Treaties on Banishment of Racial Discrimination (New York 1966) and of Discrimination of Women (New York 1979), and the Treaty for the Prevention of Torture and Inhuman or Degrading Treatment or Punishment (New York 1984).

13 Habermas (1986a, reprinted in 1991: 22) also holds this view by asserting that human rights embody generalizable interests and can – from the perspective of what everyone could want – be morally justified. They form the moral substance of the legal order.

14 See Mullen (1986: 29): '(S)uch methods of moral reasoning could readily produce arguments expressed in terms of human rights.'

15 This is why Alexy (1978) states that rational (unrestrained judicial) decision-making in a practical-legal discourse ultimately presupposes the reasonableness of lawmaking (p. 351).

16 In this respect he refers to the difference between Anglo-American and continental criminal procedure for presenting evidence (see note 5).

17 In Germany, the judiciary came to this kind of application ('Sitz-demonstration als Nötigung'), see Hassemer (1991).

18 In the Netherlands, the legislature submitted a proposal for a bill penalizing various kinds of preparatory actions. Because of this, it is now easier for the judge to presume an attempted crime.

19 As I (1988) have empirically demonstrated, using a pragmatic discourse-analysis of transcripts from criminal court cases.

20 Moreover, the grounds supporting a verdict are usually rather commonplace. For instance, in the Netherlands, it can be demonstrated that the motivations of judgments of the Dutch Supreme Court ('Hoge Raad') are becoming scanty.

21 See note 9.

22 Although these 'material' legal questions are explicitly prescribed by continental procedural law for the judge to answer, for example in the Netherlands and Germany, I believe these questions are also central in criminal procedure in common law countries.

23 Since the disclosure of subjectivity is such a common feature of every conversation (and not only explicitly by means of expressive speech-acts), the connected validity claim of sincerity inevitably plays a role.

Especially in criminal court cases, a defendant's subjective state of mind is routinely a topic of discussion. The defendant is called to account for his or her actions. In fact, the original concept of guilt is strongly related to the 'inner world' of the defendant. Although guilt is now, more and more, being determined (or ascribed) by external factors of the defendant's action and even goes in the direction of 'strict liability', the validity claim of sincerity still has its significance in forensic communication. It is of importance in discussing the acceptance of personal accountability and repentance. In this respect sincerity has its place in the ethics of responsibility ('Verantwortungsethik').

24 This will result in a broader concept of truth-finding as the main goal of criminal procedure. Truth-finding will no longer be limited to the objective determination of facts, but will encompass the establishment of 'true' moral judgement ('Wahrheitsfähigkeit praktischer Fragen').

25 In his theory of communicative action (1981), Habermas makes some interesting remarks on the principles of criminal law and procedure (p. 536). These principles as well as the basic moral concepts of crimes like murder, abortion, rape, etc., are embedded in the lifeworld. When their validity is questioned in everyday practice, a reference to their legality is insufficient. They are in need of a substantive justification, because they belong to the legitimate order of the lifeworlditself.

26 According to Habermas (1992) this is a consequence of a reverse interpretation of basic rights from deontological legal norms to teleological legal goods and values. Other than norms that claim general validity, values claim priority. Therefore, values compete for their preference. When competing values form the basis of legal decision-making, functional arguments prevail above normative arguments. In this respect, he mentions the accentuation of the functionality ('Funktionstüchtigkeit') of criminal procedure. It is my opinion that this is precisely what is going on nowadays with the emphasis on effectiveness in crime control. Normative questions on criminal law and procedure are left aside.

27 See, for example, Neumann (1989) for German criminal law and procedure.

28 See, for example, the Dutch approach to euthanasia. Although it is still a criminal act prescribed by the law, the judiciary has formulated requirements justifying non-prosecution for this type of offense. Recently, this intermediate judge-made law was included in an amendment by the legislature.

29 Except for the Netherlands, where testing a law against the Constitution is still not allowed. It is assumed to undermine the good faith in

the democratic process of lawmaking and, of course, the separation of powers. However, it is again a topic of legal debate.

30 The achievements of the Warren Court revolution in constitutional demands on criminal procedure, with regard to the 4th, 5th, 6th and 14th Amendments, are systematically brought down. Prominent legal scholars have even proposed the abrogation of the 'Miranda rules' and 'exclusionary rule' (see ' "The Miranda Report": The Law on Pretrial Interrogation, Truth in Criminal Justice', *Journal of Law Reform* [University of Michigan] 22 [3 & 4] (Spring and Summer 1989).

31 So far, the verdicts in criminal cases from the European Court in Strasburg have strengthened the position of the defendant in many respects. The court recorded several violations of human rights (mainly article 6 of the European Convention) in different national legal systems and has an important impact on changes in their procedural laws to align them more with the provisions of the European Convention.

32 An important initiative to a human rights definition of crime has already been taken by the Schwendingers (1975).

33 Meanwhile in Germany some courts held the law on marihuana-use unconstitutional on similar grounds. These cases are now before the German Constitutional Court ('Bundesverfassungsgericht').

34 According to Habermas (1991: 165) the problem of abortion does not (yet) allow for a one and only right moral answer. So far, the conflicting parties that, respectively, call upon the rights to life and to self-determination, have produced equally good and valid grounds supporting their positions. It is questionable whether this problem can be solved from a moral point of view at all, since the opposing grounds reach back to different world-views or forms of life that are – for the time being – irreconcilable. The problem of abortion can, therefore, better be solved from an ethical perspective that looks not for a rational moral consensus, but for a fair compromise between diverse ethical outlooks on life. The 'real' moral question about this issue must be raised on a more general level of a legitimate order of coexisting forms of life; how can the integrity and equal coexistence of the different world-views or life-forms be secured? I consider this the basic task of the legislature and the judiciary.

35 See the International Treaty on Economic, Social and Cultural Rights (New York 1966).

36 According to Bazelon (1988: 15–16): 'A truly moral criminal law must be guided by three fundamental principles. First, the criminal process must always remain sensitive to the social realities that underlie crime. Second, it must make meaningful the claim of "equal justice under law". Third, it must, through a process of constant

questioning, force the community to confront the painful realities and agonizing choices posed by social injustice.'

37 It should, in other words, not be accepted as a justification sui generis, by pointing at a 'rotten social background', nor as a full-blown excuse. At most it can be taken into account in the allotment of some sort of a (punitive) sanction.

38 In the Netherlands, for example, inmates have a 'constitutional' right to 'one person, one cell'. Recent proposals to place more than one prisoner in each cell because of lack of space did not succeed. They were considered a violation of the fundamental right to privacy.

Bibliography

Alexy, Robert (1978) *Theorie der juristischen Argumentation*. Frankfurt am Main: Suhrkamp.

Bal, Peter (1988) *Dwangkommunikatie in de Rechtszaal*. Arnhem: Gouda Quint.

Bazelon, David (1988) *Questioning Authority, Justice and Criminal Law*. New York: Knopf.

Bollinger, Lorenz (1992) 'German Drug Laws, Supranational Developments and Constitutionality'. Presented at the Law and Society Association annual meeting, Philadelphia.

Campbell, Thomas (1986) 'Introduction: Realizing Human Rights', in T. Campbell, D. Goldberg, S. McLean and T. Mullen (eds) *Human Rights. From Rhetoric to Reality*. Oxford: Oxford University Press.

Chambers, Simone (1992) 'Zur Politik des Diskurses: Riskieren wir unsere Rechte?', in K.-O. Apel and M. Kettner (eds) *Zur Anwendung der Diskursethik in Politik, Recht und Wissenschaft*. Frankfurt am Main: Suhrkamp.

Dworkin, Ronald (1977) *Taking Rights Seriously*. Cambridge, MA: Harvard University Press.

Dworkin, Ronald (1985) *A Matter of Principle*. Cambridge, MA: Harvard University Press.

Dworkin, Ronald (1986) *Laws' Empire*. Cambridge, MA: Harvard University Press.

Eder, Klaus (1986) 'Prozedurale Rationalität. Moderne Rechtsentwicklung jenseits von formaler Rationalisierung', *Zeitschrift für Rechtssoziologie* 7: 1.

Eder, Klaus (1988) 'Critique of Habermas's Contribution to the Sociology of Law', *Law & Society Review* 22: 931.

Ely, John (1980) *Democracy and Distrust. A Theory of Judicial Review*. Cambridge MA: Harvard University Press.

Günther, Klaus (1989) 'Ein normativer Begriff der Kohärenz für eine Theorie der juristischen Argumentation', *Rechtstheorie* 20: 163.

Günther, Klaus (1991) 'Möglichkeiten einer diskursethischen Begründung des Strafrechts', in H. Jung, H. Müller-Dietz and U. Neumann (eds) *Recht und Moral*. Baden-Baden: Nomos.

de Haan, Willem (1990) *The Politics of Redress: Crime, Punishment and Penal Abolition*. London: Allen & Unwin.

Habermas, Jürgen (1981) *Theorie des kommunikativen Handelns*, 2 vols. Frankfurt am Main: Suhrkamp.

Habermas, Jürgen (1983) *Moralbewußtsein und kommunikatives Handeln*. Frankfurt am Main: Suhrkamp.

Habermas, Jürgen (1984) 'Über Moralität und Sittlichkeit – Was macht eine Lebensform "rational"?', in H. Schnädelbach (ed.) *Rationalität*. Frankfurt am Main: Suhrkamp.

Habermas, Jürgen (1985) 'Neoconservative Culture Criticism in the United States and Western Germany: An Intellectual Movement in Two Political Cultures', in R. L. Bernstein (ed.) *Habermas and Modernity*. Cambridge: Polity Press.

Habermas, Jürgen (1986a) 'Moralität und Sittlichkeit. Treffen Hegels Einwände gegen Kant auch auf die Diskursethik zu?', in W. Kuhlmann (ed.) *Moralität und Sittlichkeit*. Frankfurt am Main: Suhrkamp.

Habermas, Jürgen (1986b) 'Gerechtigkeit und Solidarität', in W. Edelstein and G. Nunner (eds) *Bestimmung der Moralität*. Frankfurt am Main: Suhrkamp.

Habermas, Jürgen (1988) 'Law and Morality', in S. M. McMurrin (ed.) *The Tanner Lectures on Human Values*, Vol. 8. Salt Lake City: University of Utah Press.

Habermas, Jürgen (1991) *Erläuterungen zur Diskursethik*. Frankfurt am Main: Suhrkamp.

Habermas, Jürgen (1992) *Faktizität und Geltung*. Frankfurt am Main: Suhrkamp.

Hassemer, Winfried (1988) 'Menschenrechte im Strafprozeß', in J. Rüsen, E. Lämmert and P. Glotz (eds) *Die Zukunft der Aufklärung*. Frankfurt am Main: Suhrkamp.

Hassemer, Winfried (1991) 'Sozialtechnologie und Moral: Symbole und Rechtsgüter', in H. Jung, H. Müller-Dietz and U. Neumann (eds) *Recht und Moral*. Baden-Baden: Nomos.

Honneth, Axel (1986) 'Diskursethik und implizites Gerechtigkeitskonzept', in W. Kuhlmann (ed.) *Moralität und Sittlichkeit*. Frankfurt am Main: Suhrkamp.

Luhmann, Niklas (1983) *Rechtssoziologie*. Opladen: Westdeutscher Verlag.

MacCormick, Neil (1991) 'Moral Disestablishment and Rational Discourse', in H. Jung, H. Müller-Dietz and U. Neumann (eds) *Recht und Moral*. Baden-Baden: Nomos.

Mullen, Tom (1986) 'Constitutional Protection of Human Rights', in T. Campbell, D. Goldberg, S. McLean and T. Mullen (eds) *Human Rights. From Rhetoric to Reality*. Oxford: Oxford University Press.

Neumann, Ulfrid (1989) 'Materiale und prozedurale Gerechtigkeit im Strafverfahren', *Zeitschrift für die gesamte Strafrechtswissenschaft* 101: 52.

Packer, Herbert (1968) *The Limits of the Criminal Sanction*. Stanford: University of California Press.

Peters, Anthonie (1985) 'Law as Critical Discussion', in G. Teubner (ed.) *Dilemmas of Law in the Welfare State*. Berlin: Walter de Gruyter.

Peters, Anthonie (1986) 'Main Currents in Criminal Law Theory', in J. van Dijk et al. (eds) *Criminal Law in Action*. Arnhem: Gouda Quint.

Schwendinger, Herman and Schwendinger, Julia (1975) 'Defenders of Order or Guardians of Human Rights?', in I. Taylor, P. Walton and J. Young (eds) *Critical Criminology*. London: Routledge & Kegan Paul.

Weber, Max (1956) *Wirtschaft und Gesellschaft*. Tübingen: Mohr.

Bernhard Peters

On reconstructive legal and political theory

In his recent work *Faktizität und Geltung*, Habermas (1992) has presented a massive and wide-ranging theoretical interpretation of the role of law and politics in modern western societies.[1] This work represents a distinctive approach to legal phenomena and to social reality in general. Habermas himself has used the term 'reconstruction' or 'reconstructive analysis' to identify this approach. In the first part of this essay I identify some basic features of such a mode of social analysis, as I understand it. To locate this way of theorizing both in the general field of social theory and in relation to other forms of social discourse about law, I develop a typology of theoretical approaches to legal phenomena. This should clarify how reconstructive analysis relates to jurisprudential discourse and normative political theory.

Reconstructive analysis implies a certain way of treating symbols and meanings and especially certain structural features of symbolic systems and processes within the social world. I describe these features in somewhat more detail in Part II. There I also contrast reconstructive theory with another set of approaches to symbolic structures and processes which today are often labelled 'constructivist'.

In Part III we look at some actual examples of reconstructive theorizing in Habermas's latest work. His attempt to reconstruct some basic, legitimating normative principles and structures of modern legal and political orders is outlined. In my discussion I present one substantive objection: Habermas rightly insists on the importance of certain procedural principles or process values, but in doing so he treats the role of more substantive normative elements of modern constitutional orders in an ambiguous way. Part IV adds a methodological objection: the line between the empirical reconstruction of symbolic structures and a selective history of ideas or even constructive normative theorizing is sometimes blurred.

Part V finally takes up another important element of Habermas's theoretical program: reconstructive, internal analysis of symbols, meanings and symbolic processes is indispensable for social theory. But in the legal system as in every other part of the social world there are non-symbolic, non-intentional structures and mechanisms which have to be analyzed with different means, and these two modes of analysis have to be combined to get to satisfactory explanations. I try to show briefly how this applies to the legal system. Habermas's own application of this basic theoretical insight, however, is again marred by a certain ambiguity. His tendency to treat the analytical distinction between two forms of social structure (symbolic and non-symbolic; in Habermas's terms: 'social integration' and 'system integration') as an empirical distinction between different social spheres leads to certain difficulties in the treatment of legal processes. However, these difficulties seem to lead to a more adequate position, where 'systems' and 'lifeworld' appear as more intertwined and less rigidly separated. On the whole I try to demonstrate both some gains and some weaknesses of Habermas's project. As a former student of Professor Habermas, however, I follow a natural inclination to stress my disagreements somewhat more than my agreements and positive evaluations.

I Different approaches to law

As a part of our social world law is both a field of meanings and symbols (norms, principles, interpretations, etc.) and a field of social relations and social activities – namely, of all social relations which are framed in legal terms and of all activities which are specifically oriented to law. Law as a sphere of symbols and meanings is enacted, reproduced and changed by those activities. Among the defining features of modern legal systems is what is sometimes called their 'recursive' structure: the fact that the law explicitly provides for authoritative procedures and methods for making binding decisions and interpretations which determine what counts as valid law at any given time. This refers mainly to legislation and adjudication, which are the authoritative centers of all social processes that produce and reproduce law. But many more social processes are involved in the reproduction of this legal sphere: legally relevant decision-making within the political administration, the training of legal professionals, legal theorizing, the working-out of innovative legal interpretations and constructions by professionals or even laymen, broader cultural processes in which

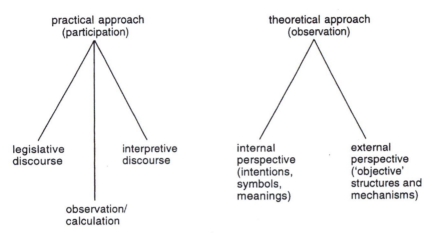

Figure 1 Approaches to law

people become acquainted with the law and develop attitudes of loyalty or opposition, and controversies in which relevant understandings of what the law is or should be are negotiated and changed. In this sense, the legal field is one of symbols and meanings, which are 'processed', so to speak, in a host of activities and communications, both formally institutionalized and not. These activities or communications can be based on several different stances toward law. Figure 1 gives a simplified typology of these stances or approaches.[2]

A practical approach to law is characterized by the practical concerns and intentions of the members of a legal community. They argue among each other what the law of the land is or should be. It is part of the special institutional characteristics of modern legal systems that these discourses fall roughly into two classes. On the one hand we have political discourses which aim at legislation – that is, at forward-looking changes in the law. The democratic nature of this political and legislative process is thought to give a mandate for this kind of deliberate legal change that is only weakly constrained by demands of consistency with pre-existing law (although often bound by constitutional provisions). On the other hand we have a multiplicity of discourses where the interpretation of pre-given law is at stake. Most importantly this takes place in the adjudication of legal claims or legally framed conflicts (in court procedures, and sometimes also in administrative procedures). But it also takes place in cases where private citizens try to figure out legal possibilities or where professionals try to systematize the law and to develop new interpretations (as in legal theory or jurisprudence). These activities, especially adjudication, are certainly a mode of changing the law itself, but one that is much more constrained (ideally) by the already existing law than is legislation.

Now there is another, quite different practical attitude toward law – a calculating, strategic one. It does not aim at understanding the demands of the law, or at convincing the other members of the legal community that the legal order should be changed in a certain way, or at striking a fair bargain about a legislative measure. Actors with a purely strategic or opportunistic attitude perceive the law merely as a set of behavioral data to which they adjust according to their own interests. In particular, they try to anticipate the reactions of legal officials or fellow citizens to their own actions in order to figure out *what they can get away with* or what *price* they will have to pay for their activities. This is the attitude of the notorious 'bad man' (Holmes, 1897: 459). Modern legal systems have to reckon with such an attitude. To a certain extent they permit or tolerate it. But it is doubtful that the practices and normative self-understandings which are institutionalized in these legal systems are solely based on a picture of the citizen as 'bad man'. It is also questionable if such an attitude is empirically dominant among citizens and legal actors and if any legal community could survive such a predominance.

In our role as social scientists, that is, within theoretical discourse, we do not act as participants in any of these senses. We suspend immediate practical intentions. Instead we try to analyze a field of meanings, communications and activities. This can be done from different perspectives and in different ways. The first important distinction is that between an 'internal' and an 'external' perspective. Within an internal perspective we take symbols, meanings, symbolic activities and the intentions, cognitions and volitions of actors into account. In the external perspective, on the other hand, we analyze objective structures, mechanisms or causal relations which are not immediately based on these symbolic elements. Theoretical approaches in the social sciences differ in the ways in which they use these two perspectives. Some of the most important examples follow.

One approach, which we might call *objectivist*, insists that *only* the external perspective is appropriate for scientific research. Its proponents regard the realm of the 'ideal' as a mere epiphenomenon or at most as an ideological reality, i.e. as an important and necessary element of the social, which, however, 'in the last instance' is determined by other social factors. Such a stance is of course represented by some branches of Marxist social theory. But there are other versions of a theoretical approach that (more or less deliberately and explicitly) refrains from dealing with meanings and intentions and bases its analyses instead on 'objective' and 'structural' factors (like 'technology', demography, or other non-symbolic features). Be-haviorism would serve as an example, but also Peter Blau's macro-social 'structural' theory (Blau, 1977; Blau, 1987; Mayhew, 1980–1). In the field of sociolegal theory, Donald Black has committed himself (at least in his programmatic statements, if not always in his actual research) to such an approach (Black, 1976).

Such extreme versions of a purely external perspective on social phenomena in general and legal phenomena in particular are not very widespread, however. Most theoretical approaches take symbolic or 'subjective' phenomena somehow into account, albeit in very different ways. One distinct approach or type of theorizing that has probably become the dominating paradigm in the social sciences for some time now I would call *strategic interactionism*. It is based on a model of intentional or meaningful action – but in a very narrow sense. Its basic elements are calculating or strategically planning actors who pursue general goals like power, status, wealth, or more specifically defined 'interests' or 'preferences'. There are 'macro' versions of this approach (like 'conflict theory'), which stress structural determinants of the strategic activities of collective actors (groups, classes), often without any deeper inquiry into the constitution of these collective actors. And there are 'micro' versions in the form of a broad class of theories on 'rational action' and 'rational choice' of individual actors. The applications of this mode of theorizing to law and politics are well known. They all presuppose that social actors basically take an opportunistic or strategic approach to the legal and political order. Equally well known are the many objections to such a theoretical perspective. Prominent among them is the criticism that these ap-proaches neglect the symbolic dimension of social life or reduce it to cognitive representations (which are largely treated as unproblematic) and certain processes of inferential reasoning and decision-making. We find attempts, of course, to give an explanation of the genesis and acceptance of norms and institutions as well as of individual 'prefer-ences' on the basis of theories of individual choice. But even in these cases the meaning of norms is reduced to social parameters, which (like prices) have to be taken into account in cost-benefit analyses, and the explanation of their development is based on the same sort of calculations.[3]

There is a further group or cluster of theories, some of them of more recent origin, which seek to rectify this neglect of the symbolic dimensions of social life. I will call them *constructivist theories*. 'Constructivism', in my usage, denotes theories which concentrate on the production and the 'processing' of meanings and symbols and which thereby attempt an analysis of the symbolic construction or constitution of reality. This constitution of reality is understood as a social process that can be studied empirically.[4] One well-known approach which uses the term 'constructivism' as a label of self-designation emerged in the field of science studies. Although it designates itself as 'new', it has strong links to older traditions in the sociology of knowledge in that it still bases its analysis on a model of intentional activity – of actors pursuing goals or 'interests' like power, status, recognition, or maybe a sense of ontological security.[5] Other approaches eschew such a notion of intentional activity directed by 'interests', and stress instead the independence and the constitutive role of symbols or symbolic processes. As the foremost current proponents of such a theoretical orientation I would regard a group of theorists who call their paradigm 'radical constructivism' or 'autopoietic' systems theory. Niklas Luhmann is their most prolific representative. The nature of Luhmann's work is often misunderstood because of misleading associations with earlier versions of 'systems theory'. It is important to see that his work has stronger links to other versions of what I call 'constructivist' approaches; examples are social phenomenology (Alfred Schütz), most versions of ethnomethodology, structuralism (especially in its linguistic or semiotic versions) and discourse analysis. These theoretical orientations have several significant features in common: a *genetic* perspective on processes of constitution or construction; an emphasis on the determining role of symbolic deep structures (modes or categories of experience, codes, grammars, sign systems, semantics) within these processes; and finally a certain descriptive or objectivating theoretical attitude which 'brackets' the *validity* of these symbolic processes (or the role of validity claims that are raised within them). This last feature is often connected with the assumption that there are basic discontinuities or separations between distinct symbolic fields or discourses, including a radical discontinuity between the discourse of social science itself and the other social discourses as object of its study.[6]

Finally, we come to still another theoretical orientation, which is the main topic of this article. Lacking a better term I call it 'reconstructive'.[7] A *reconstructive social theory* has some commonalities with constructivist approaches. Like them, reconstructive theories analyse the symbolic dimension, especially processes of symbolic production and reproduction and their underlying structures. Reconstructive theories, however, take a performative attitude or an internal perspective with respect to the symbolic processes that they study. They do not bracket validity claims, but take them seriously and give them certain explanatory functions. This distinctive trait of reconstructive analysis is described in the next paragraph.

II Reconstructive legal analysis

In reconstructive legal analysis we try to describe which legal rules the members (or different parts of the membership) follow, how they go about using, interpreting and changing them, for what reasons they accept or reject a legal order or parts of it as binding. In order to do this we have to grasp these meanings as they are articulated and understood by the participants. But we are not bound to stay entirely within the horizon of understanding or self-understanding that is present in everyday discourses, and in any case we are not interested in simply describing them or making an inventory of them. Reconstructive analysis will transcend or widen this horizon in several directions. One of these directions is the search for underlying symbolic structures within the totality of legal meanings and interpretations that is found in social beliefs and discourses: systematic connections, normative and cognitive models or paradigms, presuppositions or background assumptions that are not explicitly articulated in practical legal discourses, but that are discernible and that may have some unreflected directive functions within these discourses.[8] These are elements of the collective unconscious, or unreflected, implicit symbolic surroundings of more articulate beliefs and more explicit meanings of communications. Bringing them out will not necessarily overturn those beliefs. But it will make them more reflective and discriminating – and thereby possibly more open to criticism. This is less true for other discoveries that a reconstructive inquiry may produce: it may come upon inconsistencies and the denial of these. It may find distortions in communication, manipulation, or resigned acceptance of a legal order which seems unchangeable. It may discover forms of collective self-deception, hidden motives, collective mythologies, prejudices and stereotypes that are resistant or immune to critical reflection and questioning. Such conclusions, if accepted by the social actors themselves, would immediately change their self-understandings and social definitions.

In order to make such diagnoses meaningful, theorists must be able to apply criteria of rationality or reasonableness to the beliefs and activities they study which are valid not only for themselves but potentially also for the social actors they study. Only if we presuppose something like a continuum of rationality and reasonableness between the field of social science and other social fields and practices can we reach this particular kind of rational understanding and explanation. Only then can we distinguish between explanations that rely on the force of reason in the social world itself and other forms of explanation by external causes (domination, manipulation, contingent circumstances or perhaps external 'material' factors). Only then can we say that certain activities were undertaken because actors had good reasons for them, or that certain changes in belief systems or in normative orders represent genuine insights or the result of learning processes. And only then can we maintain (as Habermas does) that social interaction based on language and the attempt to reach mutual understanding contains not only a *potential* for learning but also a *constraint* (because genuine insights cannot be changed, retracted, or denied *at will*) and a *stimulus*, an irritation, an impulse to argue, to question pre-given beliefs and understandings in the search for better understandings that may be convincing for all.[9] The presupposition that basic principles of rationality and validity can be shared between observer (theorist) and participant (social actor) implies a certain symmetrical relationship between them – a principle of epistemic symmetry. Theorists try to understand their 'subjects' or the cultural elements they are dealing with in a way not *principally* different from their attempts to understand other theorists or theories (empirical or normative). And the participants are able in principle to understand and criticize what the theorists have to say about them. There would be technical difficulties, of course, but there is no fundamental epistemological barrier.[10]

Whether these forms of rational reconstruction and explanation are possible and desirable is of course still debatable. This debate leads to difficult arguments about meaning, understanding and the universality of rationality and symbolic validity (Habermas, 1988). I will confine myself here to one argument. The reconstructive theorist who analyses symbolic structures and activities in the social world in the way described can apply the same mode of analysis *to her own practice*. She can account within her theory for the status of her own theoretical enterprise *without being inconsistent* in her self-understanding. As a theorist she presents arguments and evidence in order to convince others. In addressing others in such a way, she presupposes that she can move them to accept her claims on rational grounds (she also sees herself as convinced on rational grounds that her claims have merit). In doing so she gives reason, argument, or insight at least a potentially explanatory role, even if she knows about all the contingent circumstances on which the development and acceptance of theoretical claims also depend. She could not, for example, describe all forms of argumentation as a strategic attempt to gain power without throwing doubt on the status of her own theoretical claims and without a split consciousness with regard to her own activities. 'Constructivists' seem to run into just this kind of problem. If they 'bracket' in principle the validity of symbol systems or the validity claims of social actors and therefore deny any explanatory force to reason or insight (as they generally do), they deny with respect to the symbolic processes they study what they presuppose in their own theoretical activity. This kind of objection is by no means new, of course. With respect to the sociology of knowledge and especially with respect to 'constructivist' theories of science it has often been argued that an 'external' approach to symbolic practices such as science, which regards them merely as social games about status, power or other such goals, or in terms of merely contingent symbolic codes or structures, undermines its own claim – the claim, that is, to be taken for more than just another attempt at manipulation or just another symbolic game.[11] The argument has not convinced the 'constructivists'.[12] But I think it is valid and applicable not only to the social study of science but also to the study of other fields of symbolic activity – if we don't want to take Karl Mannheim's escape: to claim a privileged epistemic position for science (or for intellectuals), which sets scientific discourse totally apart from, for example, political or legal discourse.

By way of illustration, some recent works in the field of law, morality and politics can be mentioned which represent at least some important features of what I described as a reconstructive approach. Notable examples of a search for central principles, paradigms or conceptual structures that underlie changes in the law are recent studies by Henry Steiner (Steiner, 1987), Lawrence Friedman (Friedman, 1985; 1990), Robert Post (see below) and Kim Scheppele (Scheppele, 1988). Friedman looks for changing cultural values, such as changing interpretations of the principle of justice and of a right to personal choice and self-fulfillment, that represent an implicit, unifying conceptual thread in recent developments of American law. Steiner looks at changing 'social visions' and moral conceptions within the field of tort jurisprudence. Robert Post has in a series of articles (Post, 1986, 1988, 1989, 1990) tried to show that conflicting conceptions of the nature of social relations are implicit in the jurisprudence of communication law. And Kim Scheppele compares how different paradigms – a 'law and economics' model and a contractarian normative interpretation – work as a reconstruction of principles which direct the jurisprudence about secrecy and disclosure. Other examples are the numerous studies by members of the 'Critical Legal Studies' movement who try to uncover conflicting principles or social visions at the base of modern law.

Jürgen Habermas and Wolfgang Schluchter have both given a more abstract structural analysis of modern law in general. They have tried to show how stages in legal development presuppose or incorporate stages in the development of normative rationality. Both have attempted a reformulation of Max Weber's work on the development of modern ethics and law. Schluchter made use of Lawrence Kohlberg's theory of moral development in ontogeny, with its scheme of successive stages of increasingly complex and rational moral competence. According to Schluchter, one could fit Max Weber's somewhat ambiguous descriptions of the 'rationalization' of occidental law and ethics into a similar developmental scheme (Schluchter, 1979: 148). Habermas, while more critical of Weber's original account, also took Kohlberg's studies as a model. He tried to show how phylogenetic developments in the areas of ethics, law and legitimate political orders followed a developmental logic, where successive stages of increasingly universal and rational symbolic structures provided necessary (but not sufficient) conditions for institutional innovations, like the development of legitimate political orders and finally of modern constitutional regimes (Habermas, 1979; 1984: Ch. 2).[13]

Habermas's recent writings are a renewed effort of such a rational reconstruction, this time applied more specifically to structures and developments within modern law. In the following two parts of this article I will offer some comments on this attempt.

III Habermas's reconstructive analysis of democracy and modern law: some comments

In his recent work Professor Habermas tries to reconstruct the symbolic, basic or 'deep' structure of our modern legal and political orders, something like the symbolic core of this historical enterprise of building constitutional, democratic states and legal regimes. In this attempt he basically takes a process perspective: like the adherents of a 'constructivist' approach, he is primarily looking at *generative* principles or structures – at the ways, that is, in which processes of symbolic production and reproduction are themselves symbolically structured. The starting-point of Habermas's inquiry is an analysis of the processes of social coordination, collective will-formation and conflict resolution. In his *Theory of Communicative Action* he developed a model of social coordination through speech-acts. In this mode of coordination actors develop shared understandings and agreements in different dimensions of symbolic validity (truth, authenticity, moral rightness). Elaborating on this he has more recently sketched out a typology of practical discourses by which joint action can be achieved on the basis of reasoned consent, that is, without force or manipulation (Habermas, 1991: 100–18; 1989b; 1992). He distinguishes several types of practical discourse: pragmatic discourse, which seeks the most efficient relations between a multiplicity of means and ends; ethical-political discourse, where definitions of collective identity and conceptions of the good life are at stake; and moral discourse about the impartial consideration of competing claims. Two further distinctions cut across this typology: there is a distinction between discourses, in which general norms are *justified* with regard to typical problems or situations where they might apply, and discourses where such general norms are *applied* to specific actual cases.[14] And finally: not all conflicts are resolvable by discourse and reasoned agreement; there are cases where we find no objective criteria for resolution and resort instead to bargaining and compromise. The legitimacy of compromises is, on Habermas's account, dependent on the fairness of the conditions under which these compromises were reached.

In the modern world, this mode of coordination by reasoned agreement or alternatively by fair compromise becomes more important, both as a normative ideal of collective autonomy or self-determination and as a practice of disputing. Modes of social integration that are based on unquestioned and unified traditions and on mythical or metaphysical beliefs which are dogmatically held and shielded against criticism, are undermined. But agreement is difficult to achieve through unregulated discourse, and actors cannot always safely rely on it afterwards. To achieve binding collective decisions in time, to support them, if necessary, through the application of sanctions, and to organize the implementation of collective plans, it is necessary to institutionalize the various modes of practical discourses in legal and political forms. The deliberative formation of collective convictions and intentions has to be made effective by political power – but the legitimacy of power itself is generated in these discursive processes. The modern legal and political association is not only a community of rights-bearing persons who grant each other equal rights and liberties on moral grounds. It is also a form of organized, instrumental social cooperation and to some degree also an ethical community with common values and aspirations for the life of the community as a whole. Its legitimacy accordingly has to be created by a combination of the different kinds of discourse which were mentioned above. Habermas maintains that the specific character of each type of practical discourse as well as the conditions of fair compromise imply certain principles of procedure which are to some degree realized in the form of constitutional provisions, e.g. in specific regulations for legislation, adjudication and the control of public administration. This is (apart from some institutional elements which will be mentioned below) the basic normative structure of the modern democratic 'Rechtsstaat', according to Habermas.[15]

On reconstructive legal and political theory

Habermas's analysis contains many interesting elements and important insights. His conception of practical discourse and compromise provides for an understanding of democratic, 'deliberative' politics which overcomes the widespread, narrow understanding of politics as mere aggregation of private interests.[16] His distinction between the 'moral' and 'ethical' elements of politics, between principles of justice and evaluative conceptions of a collective life-form with common aspirations and projects, lets him keep a healthy distance from the more problematic elements of 'communitarian' or 'republican' understandings of modern society and politics. Habermas rightly insists that the modern development of social and cultural diversity or pluralism cannot be replaced by a new unitary conception of the collective 'good life' (as some communitarians seem to presuppose). But he equally rightly maintains that the pluralism of 'ethical' life-forms is compatible with unity and consensus regarding basic constitutional principles and procedures. Modern legal and political orders provide the unity which makes difference possible (*FG*: 640–3).

Here I will concentrate on certain aspects of Habermas's position which seem to be in need of clarification. Habermas identifies a certain notion of collective freedom and a corresponding notion of legitimacy as the normative core of our modern democratic conceptions of law and politics. A political community (within the bounds of the modern nation-state) conducts its affairs in an autonomous and authentic way if it is able to form common convictions and a collective 'will' by way of open, unrestricted, egalitarian discourse, if it is able to find solutions to problems or conflicts on the basis of rational argument or fair compromise. Another condition is that there be suitable procedures and provisions for channeling collective deliberations into specific decisions and for controlling the proper implementation of such decisions. *Legitimacy* of collective decision procedures and outcomes is achieved if the procedures guarantee collective deliberations (of the kind described) and if the outcomes can be understood by the participants as compatible with the results of these deliberations. To them, these outcomes must seem acceptable in the light of the arguments that were provided in these public debates. There is obviously a logical connection between these notions of collective freedom and legitimacy: the same set of conditions, i.e. certain conditions of public deliberation and the making and implementation of collective decisions, makes for both freedom and legitimacy. In addition there is a conceptual link between the notions of freedom (or autonomy) and legitimacy on the one hand and the notion of rationality or reason on the other: reason (or 'communicative rationality', as Habermas says) becomes reality in public deliberation. And unconstrained deliberation provides for the rationality (or, as Habermas sometimes says, the 'presumption of rationality') of its outcomes. All this amounts in a way to a procedural concept of popular sovereignty which is meant to solve Rousseau's problem of the transformation of the *volonté de tous* into the *volonté générale*. But the solution is different from the one that Rousseau himself imagined. Not some mysterious social alchemy, but the conditions of public deliberation and discursive institutional procedures are to guarantee that the popular will becomes also the enlightened will.[17]

Much of this would need further explication and examination, of course. Here I will only comment on some conceptual aspects which I find somewhat unclear or ambiguous, and then point to some problems with respect to the general character of 'reconstruction' in Habermas's latest work.

From the principles of collective freedom and legitimacy and from his analysis of the several types of public discourse and decision-making by which public freedom is realized and legitimacy generated, Habermas derives certain institutional principles for democratic and legal *procedures and processes*. Among them are, for example, certain normative constraints on the division of functions and competences between the processes of legislation, adjudication and public administration. In his view, constitutional orders in modern democratic states do partially realize or at least acknowledge these demands. To the degree that they fail to do so, they are inconsistent with their own basic legitimizing principles.

Many of these 'process principles' make good sense. A first difficulty, however, is the problem of the 'second best': what to do if the institutional solution which is 'ideally' right or justified cannot be implemented as such? How to find the next best institutional design? Even under optimal conditions, processes of democratic deliberation and decision-making will to a certain degree be distorted. Above all they will be very limited in their capacity to deal with the enormous complexity of political and legal problems. Habermas himself certainly recognizes the many empirical constraints on the realization of democratic self-government in modern societies and is very careful to avoid naive normative conceptions. But given this, is it still possible to derive normative demands for legal and political institutions directly from basic normative principles, the way he does it? To give a simple example: the principle of democratic sovereignty requires that courts apply the law, but do not genuinely create new law. But given all the unavoidable imperfections of the democratic process, might not, under some circumstances, the delegation of certain law-making capacities to the courts be justified? Would it not be more appropriate to compare the capacities or capabilities of institutions and procedures under given historical circumstances and define their competences accordingly, rather than just to 'deduce' these competencies from basic principles?

I will not pursue this line of questioning, however, but point to a different difficulty. Thus far we talked only about 'process values'. Now, we find in modern constitutional, legal and political orders many normative principles which are regarded as valuable or justifiable quite independently from their role for democratic processes. Among them are protections of personal integrity against interference by others (or by the state), equal rights and liberties that give people protected social spaces to develop and realize their individual and collective life-plans, certain protections for the weak or needy, some forms of equality of resources or life-chances. These and similar normative principles might be justified in a number of ways, and there are a number of normative theories around which try to do this. But certainly such justifications do not solely rely on their role as preconditions for democratic participation. Habermas acknowledges as much. In his latest book he gives these human rights a somewhat complicated two-step treatment. In the first step he conducts a thought experiment: given that prospective citizens wanted to found a legal-political order, i.e. an institutional order that provides for binding collective decisions and their enforcement, if necessary, by way of sanctions (or threat of force), which basic rights would they have to grant each other to make this a *legitimate* order (FG: 151–60)? Since the principles of legitimation which were described above already presuppose the existence of such a community, Habermas's argument here relies on a more general notion of legitimacy which can be found in his principle of unconstrained universal agreement or 'discourse principle' (FG: 138). This principle states that general norms are valid if and only if they could be accepted by all concerned as participants in rational discourse.[18] Habermas concludes that under this hypothetical condition the prospective citizens would grant each other a 'system of rights' which includes equal liberties, equal access to fair judicial procedures, regulations of membership, rights to political participation and basic welfare rights. This is a minimal condition: in order to pass the test of hypothetical universal agreement, every legal-political order would need to have these formal features. The specific contents of these rights and regulations are still open at this stage. Now this derivation may be convincing or not – what concerns me here is Habermas's second step: there he goes on to argue that the specific contents of the system of rights should be determined in processes of public deliberation and democratic decision-making (*FG*: 161–3). This was already implied by his concept of collective freedom, of course. In addition he seems to maintain that the specific rights become legitimate only *as products* of deliberative political processes. It is not obvious exactly what this means. Does it mean that a constitutional order with individual rights and 'negative' liberties is somehow incomplete and of questionable legitimacy without rights to democratic participation? This seems uncontroversial. Does it mean that individual liberties cannot be safe without public freedom? This is an empirical claim with considerable appeal. Does it mean that open public debate on the content of these rights and liberties is important? This seems a plausible and significant principle. Does it mean that all these rights and liberties should be subject to regular democratic decision-making? This appears to be a more difficult question, which cannot be answered without regard for institutional details (e.g. the role of institutional self-limitations). Does it mean finally that 'negative' rights and liberties are of no real value as long as they are not the actual result of democratic decision-making and not complemented by democratic rights? This seems implausible. If we could force a dictatorship to grant basic human rights, even without granting democratic participation, would this not be worthwhile? This example is outside the scope of Habermas's discussion. But it shows that we have reason to value rights and liberties somewhat independently of their connection with democracy. If we try to analyse the central normative principles which underlie our modern constitutional orders, we have to give some independent weight to conceptions of 'negative' liberty and dignity, justice and solidarity – even if we find other basic principles which demand that the content of these conceptions should be developed in public discourse. Habermas does not want to treat human rights as a mere precondition for rights of political participation. Instead he claims that these two sorts of rights are 'complementary' (*FG*: 503). It is not entirely clear to me what kind of connection this means.[19] His intricate treatment of these conceptual relations may still show a tendency to put all good things (or too many) into a strong concept of democracy.

Another way to look at the relations between procedural principles and other elements of modern legal and political systems is to ask: How does the legitimacy or rational acceptability of collectively binding decisions depend on the procedures by which these decisions were generated? We can distinguish several possibilities. There are procedural regulations which make possible or protect open, unrestricted deliberation which may lead to common convictions and agreements. In this case, acceptance of the results is based on the arguments or reasons that were produced in the process. Participants are

On reconstructive legal and political theory

Table 1 Procedural legitimacy

Category	Definition	Example
Perfect procedural legitimacy	process-independent criteria, but procedure guarantees correct outcomes	ideal discourse
Imperfect procedural legitimacy	process-independent criteria, procedures further correct and thereby produce trustworthy outcomes	professional institutions (medicine, science)
Pure procedural legitimacy	no process-independent criteria for acceptability of outcomes	lotteries, competitions
Quasi-pure procedural legitimacy	process-independent criteria; procedures further correct outcomes; process-based criteria have independent, additional weight	court procedures, democratic process

convinced 'on the merits', so to speak. The process of deliberation may have been a facilitative or even necessary condition for producing and evaluating these arguments and thereby for producing grounded convictions. From the standpoints of the participants this means that they can trust their own judgements more if they have tested them in critical discussion, if no viewpoint was excluded, if everybody was given a voice and a hearing, and so on. But in the end it must still be the substance of the arguments that provides a basis for rational judgements. It is not the character of the procedure as such that makes the outcome acceptable.

But there are cases where the acceptance of outcomes is based on an evaluation of the procedure itself. Let us distinguish types of relations between procedures and the legitimacy or acceptability of their outcomes. Let us call them perfect and imperfect, pure and quasi-pure procedural legitimacy.[20] Table 1 gives a summary of these distinctions.

In *pure procedural legitimacy*, there are no independent substantive grounds for the acceptance or rejection of an outcome. Everything depends on the fairness or acceptability of the procedure itself. Lotteries or competitions could be examples. In *perfect* as well as in *imperfect procedural legitimacy* there are substantive criteria or reasons for the acceptability of outcomes. Perfect procedures would guarantee that the outcome is always in accordance with these criteria. They would always produce the 'one right answer'. Maybe an ideal, 'infinite' and 'unrestricted' discourse would fulfil this definition (that was Peirce's idea). Discourses under real world conditions can never *guarantee* such an outcome. Real procedures, however, can have features that make them suitable for producing good or correct outcomes – for instance, by forcing the participants to produce and examine reasons or apply given criteria and make this the basis of the outcome. This would make it possible, especially for non-participants, to accept the outcome *not* 'on the merits', but based on their trust in the procedure itself. They would suspend their own judgements on the merits of the case and would rely on the expectation that the procedure, if properly followed by the participants, is likely enough to produce good results. (This we do all the time in our daily life; for instance, if we rely on scientific results that we could never check ourselves.) But it would in principle always be possible to question such an outcome on substantive grounds. In *quasi-pure procedural legitimacy*, there is an additional element. Here we have procedures that we trust in the just mentioned sense – in that we think that they will produce acceptable results, at least in general or in the long run. But we also regard the results as *binding* – even in most cases where we think they are substantively wrong. This we do because we have committed ourselves beforehand, in one way or another, to accept the results or because we think that these procedures are the best form to regulate some of our collective affairs, so that we are willing to accept occasional mistakes or wrong outcomes because we think they will get corrected in the long run or that it is worth paying the price of occasional mishaps. But we reserve judgement, so to speak: if the mistake seems too serious, we might refuse to go along, even if the procedure followed is unexceptionable. I think this is the most fitting description of the most common normative attitude toward legal and political procedures – particularly voting and legislation as well as adjudication. There might be additional elements: in some cases, for instance, we would make certain procedural features a *necessary* condition for the acceptability of an outcome (if we insist, for instance, that the parties to a court case are given a hearing). But in general we either operate on the basis of trust in procedures, or as participants we are ready to submit to the final decision (a majority decision, for instance) regardless of our own substantive conviction. In certain cases, however, we may well feel justified by our own substantive convictions in not obeying a law or a court decision, even if all the procedural rules were followed without a flaw. That means: only in cases of pure procedural legitimacy do we actually rely on the procedure alone. So if we analyse principles of legitimacy in modern societies, we should not only look for procedural principles. We should also consider if there is a basic stock of common viewpoints, convincing reasons, or substantive normative conceptions. Even if these conceptions have to be regarded as fallible, always subject to further debate, criticism and revision, they are what legal and political communities have to live by in any given period.[21] Empirically we might of course find that no common normative principles exist in a given case. But then the whole concept of legitimation as developed so far would not be applicable.

To put the main argument of this paragraph more generally: we might well say (with Habermas) that what marks a modern worldview as rational, and institutions like science, law and politics as rational enterprises, is not any substantive insight or achievement, but a general openness to argument and criticism or the reliance on certain forms of open discourse. From the standpoint of the *participants* at any given historical moment, however, it is obviously not this feature alone, but it is still the convincing force of substantive arguments that (ideally or rationally) leads them to accept certain propositions as true, certain norms or institutional orders as legitimate. And a reconstructive analysis of such a legitimate order cannot leave out the description and assessment of these substantive reasons and principles.

IV Tensions between normative and empirical theory

This discussion may have provoked some doubts about the character of Habermas's enterprise. Is this really a reconstructive analysis (in the sense explained) or is it largely a work of normative legal and political theory? The question points to some methodological difficulties of reconstructive theorizing. If we look at the law or any other symbolic field in modern societies, we find that social definitions and understandings are rarely stable, unequivocal and systematic. Instead we find semantic fields with shifting and disputed meanings, controversial and 'contested concepts', ambiguities and inconsistencies, and complex configurations of consent and dissent, of concurrent and competing interpretations. Of course, cultural fields can be unified or segmented in different ways and to different degrees, but a large degree of homogeneity does not seem typical for our societies. This fact does not necessarily invalidate a program of theoretical reconstruction. It may well be possible, for instance, to identify some common basic structures that underlie many of the surface differences, or certain 'hegemonic' or 'official' conceptions that have some legitimating function. Habermas attempts to reconstruct something like a coherent set of very basic and abstract normative conceptions which are implicit in our modern world-view and in our legal and political traditions and institutions. This deep structure appears at the surface of actual beliefs, communications and practices only in blurred and refracted ways, often in incoherent mixtures with different conceptions. But still Habermas claims some actual force for these basic principles (like the principle of collective freedom and legitimacy). According to him, they are at least partially acknowledged in constitutional provisions and in legal and political practices, and they motivate attempts to criticize and revise these practices. Such attempts at describing some basic symbolic structures of legal and political institutions and cultures can certainly be illuminating and useful, even if at first done in a very general and tentative way. There is, however, a fine line between reconstructive analysis in the sense described here and a different form of theoretical 'reconstruction'. In this second form we do not look primarily for symbolic structures that were actually operative in a certain region of the social world during a certain time period. Instead we search certain traditions of philosophical, political or legal thought or even our practical, everyday convictions or intuitions for conceptual elements that could be reassembled or reconfigured to a coherent and normatively convincing theoretical conception (of morality and law, for instance). This may well be a valid enterprise that could even be said to bring out some latent truth in the cultural traditions under study. But it is nevertheless a primarily *normative* discourse, not an empirical reconstruction. Habermas seems to shift between these two modes of analysis; in fact, his latest work often seems closer to the second mode. But even a philosophical analysis of this type can provide important *hypotheses* for reconstruction: we can try to show that certain philosophical conceptions express symbolic meanings that are to a certain degree incorporated in the general culture and in social institutions. In this sense, Habermas's work gives interesting and important leads for more empirical reconstructions.

V Internal and external perspectives: the law between 'systems' and 'lifeworld'?

So far we have discussed only certain aspects of an *internal* perspective on the *symbolic* dimensions of legal and political systems. However, such an internal, reconstructive approach needs to be complemented by other empirical forms of analysis. Law is a field of intentional activities and beliefs where legal symbols or meanings are the objects of such beliefs or intentions and where such symbols and meanings are communicated, interpreted, changed, created, passed on. If we try to analyze how this whole process works, the interpretation and reconstructive analysis of these meanings and symbolic structures certainly has to play an important part. The most common and most easily understood way in which interpretive analysis serves for explanatory purposes is *intentional explanation*, where we try to explain activities by referring to the reasons the actors presumably had for undertaking them. Reconstructive analysis, however, attempts more than this. It tries to analyze the whole symbolic sphere that serves as the background of these specific reasons. In a reconstructive analysis we try to uncover systematic connections within such a symbolic sphere, underlying structures, constitutive categories, presuppositions, generative rules, none of which is normally reflected on consciously by the participants themselves, although they might in principle be able to articulate it. Finally we might be able to identify distortions, inconsistencies, dogmatic or self-immunizing forms of beliefs and communication.[22] But all this does not give us a sufficient explanation of how the legal field is structured, how it reproduces itself, or how the activities that make up this field are regulated. If we look at legal and political institutions and processes we have a strong sense that there are other, non-intentional, 'material' factors or 'objective' structures at work, which have to be analyzed differently.

This becomes more obvious if we look outside the legal and political sphere itself. Evidently the reproduction of the legal field is influenced by processes in other social spheres, while the law itself provides parts of the regulating structure within these other social areas. If we look at such areas – for instance, the economy or science – we again see structures and regulating mechanisms of different kinds: there are symbolic structures (legal norms among them). But there are also other mechanisms. This is most obvious with respect to the economy, where market mechanisms provide a widely recognized form of non-intentional regulation. But it could be shown also for science that such non-symbolic forms of structuring (for instance, certain organizational processes or again certain market mechanisms) play a role. Also if we look at the interdependencies between these different social spheres, we find them to be of two different kinds: there are influences that operate in the symbolic dimension, for instance where scientific discoveries or changes in moral value lead to legal change. And there are external, non-symbolic influences, for instance where the dynamics of economic development create social conditions which result in legal problems or demands for legal change.

Habermas has made a distinction between different modes of social regulation and a corresponding distinction between two forms of theoretical analysis a cornerstone of his work. He contrasts 'social integration' with 'system integration' as two basic mechanisms of social coordination, or 'lifeworld' with 'system' as social spheres which are constituted by these two mechanisms. Social integration is based on intentional, symbolically constituted relations – communications, intentional interactions, common beliefs, legitimate norms, relations of trust and solidarity, collective identities as well as disputes and conflicts. Personal domination and coercion do of course occur within the lifeworld, but Habermas sees them more as pathologies within a field of normative relationships. System integration, on the other hand, consists in non-symbolic, objective functional interdependencies or the unplanned, unintended linkage of the results of intentional activities. While social integration requires an internal, interpretive or recon-structive analysis, the mechanisms of system integration can be grasped only by an empirical-analytical (or 'functional') analysis. These are valid and useful distinctions.

His analysis goes on in a more problematic direction, however. According to him, these two modes of social coordination have come to constitute separated social spheres in modern societies. The modern economy and the modern state have become demarcated systems which are 'uncoupled' or 'disembedded' from the lifeworld. They are essentially regulated by non-intentional mechanisms which are not based on mutual understanding but work 'behind the backs' of the actors. Habermas speaks of 'money' and 'power' as 'steering media' which bring about this kind of coordination (thereby adopting a term that was used by Parsons and Luhmann). This seems hardly more than a suggestive metaphor, however. In any case, Habermas has been mostly content with this general characterization and has generally left the 'systems' to the 'systems theorists'. The lifeworld, on the other hand, which is reproduced by communicative action, has itself become rationalized. This means, in Habermas's usage, that world-views or systems of cultural categories have become differentiated and new levels of critical reflection, learning and discursive testing of inherited beliefs or normative orders are possible.[23]

Now, it is just this rationalization of the lifeworld that has made the emergence of the modern market economy and the modern state and their detachment from the lifeworld possible. Here the law has a crucial mediating function in Habermas's theoretical model. The development of modern formal law presupposes and incorporates universalistic and 'postconventional' moral conceptions. At the same time, the law institutionalizes the 'media' of money and power and thereby helps constitute the social systems as spheres of social action where normative integration becomes effectively neutralized. In his more recent writings Habermas has stressed this mediating function. The law serves as some kind of pivot or transmission-belt between lifeworld and systems. The lifeworld is the (potential) site of a loosely connected network of non-institutionalized discourses in which collective self-reflection and self-definition take place. The law institutionalizes the channels (in the form of political and legal procedures) and provides a language or medium (in the form of binding norms) through which the results of these informal deliberative processes can become socially binding and effective – and can to a certain degree constrain and regulate the 'systems' (*FG*: 399–467).

This construct, however, sits somewhat uncomfortably between 'system' and 'lifeworld'. If legal and political procedures can have this channeling and mediating function, what is left of the alleged uncoupling or separateness of the 'systems', especially the state (or the political-administrative system), and of the alleged absence of normative integration in this domain? In this way, 'systems' must at least be permeable by normative influences. And what about the legal sphere, the democratic 'Rechtsstaat' or the system of political and legal discourses itself? Is it 'system' or 'lifeworld' or something in between? And what about other fields of specialized social activity, like science or health care – which are formally organized and separate, but hardly void of symbolic integration? Most plausibly all these social fields or spheres of social action should be regarded as made up both by forms of 'social integration' and of 'system integration' – that is, by intentional and symbolic structures and mechanisms and by non-intentional and non-symbolic forms of social order. And there is enough evidence that the same is true, for example, for the economic system (that is, for markets and organizations) and for political administrations.[24] How much or how little social integration there is within the economy or the political system should therefore be treated as an empirical question and not be decided *a priori*. In his latest book, Habermas himself seems to make a step in that direction.

One way in which the dualism of system and lifeworld nevertheless reappears in Habermas's recent writings is that 'non-institutionalized discourses' take up a privileged position (*FG*: 435–67).[25] These informal processes of opinion formation and possibly of critical discussion are undoubtedly important. But why are they depicted as the prime source of social wisdom and as untainted by the competition for power or other distorting influences which (in this picture) make more formally institutionalized discourses less suitable for rational problem-solving? In fact, the 'informal' discourses that I know – such as intellectual circles, specialized cultural and political publics, or social movements – definitely have their share of unconscious structures and mechanisms, of cultural blinders, selective perception, status competition, distorted communication and so on. Perhaps these influences are less distorting than in party politics, jurisprudence, or administrative agencies or other forms of 'institutionalized' discourse, but this is an open empirical question. Similar things could be said for other areas of 'informal' social relations.

From these considerations I draw the conclusion that we should treat the distinction between social integration and system integration strictly as analytical – as a distinction between modes or mechanisms of social coordination which can be combined and intertwined within real life-forms in many ways, and not as the basis for the demarcation of separate social spheres. The analytical distinction should probably be differentiated further. There are forms of intentional coordination, either consensual (as in communicatively achieved agreements or compromises or in the common orientation to norms which are considered legitimate) or strategic (as in competition or certain forms of conflict). There is the influence of symbolic forms or structures which are not consciously reflected on. There are forms of ideology in the sense of 'false consciousness' (not simply error, but distortions in reasoning or communication and the inability or refusal to correct them). There is the delegation of decisions or judgements either to procedures or to persons (or collective bodies) which are trusted or in a position of institutional authority or otherwise in a position of power. (This is a most pervasive structure in modern society which not only pertains to what is normally conceived as power or authority relations, but also to more or less reciprocal relationships.) And there are forms of indirect coordination, based on unplanned linkages and interdependencies between independent activities: serial links, either temporal (as in adaptations to the results, material or other ways, of earlier activities) or in the social dimension (networks). There are aggregation effects of multiple independent activities, and there are forms of mutual adaptation between actors (where every actor treats the decisions or actions of all others as given and adapts his or her own behavior accordingly). These forms of indirect coordination can create

On reconstructive legal and political theory

Table 2 Social relations and mechanisms in the reproduction of law

| | Internal | | External |
	Intentional, symbolic	Non-intentional, symbolic	Non-intentional, non-symbolic
Inside the legal field	1	2	3
Outside the legal field	4	5	6

complex patterns and configurations; markets are only the most famous example. All these mechanisms are very much intertwined in *all* areas of social life. There is no real divide, in this respect, between small groups and large organizations. The mixture or configuration can vary, of course, as can the degree to which something like deliberate or conscious collective regulation of a social field can be achieved. But this is always a matter of degree.

Legal norms, as far as they regulate behavior, are a form of intentional, symbolic social order. How important such a common orientation to law is in our present society, what the grounds for the acceptance of a legal order are – convictions about its substantive merits (as being just, reasonable, etc.), some form of procedural legitimation, as described above, resigned acceptance, or even a mere calculating 'bad man' perspective – all these are open empirical possibilities. If we look on the other hand at all the social processes in which the legal field is reproduced, we can safely say that we have here just such a mixture of mechanisms as mentioned above: discursive processes in many different social and political arenas, bargains, forms of indirect (or 'systemic') coordination in the shape of political networks that try to influence legislation or in bureaucratic processes within political administrations, and so on. Table 2 gives (just as a reminder) a simple classification of these different types of social relations and mechanisms involved in the reproduction of the legal sphere. All these different types of elements are combined in all other social areas as well (although always in different constellations).

'Intentional symbolic relations' are reasons, motives, beliefs, convictions of actors that are more or less conscious or articulated. 'Non-intentional symbolic relations' are symbolic structures and assumptions that stay 'in the background' or make up the 'cultural unconscious' of a society. (These two categories roughly correspond to

Habermas's notion of 'social integration'; the corresponding phenomena are the subject-matter of reconstructive analysis.) Non-intentional and non-symbolic mechanisms work 'behind the backs' of the actors in the various ways I have just mentioned (in Habermas's terminology they are forms of 'system integration'). These various factors can originate either inside or outside a given social sphere. What the specific mixture and the respective influence of these factors are, I shall again not discuss here. My point so far is only that we should choose a conceptual framework that is open to these empirical alternatives.

These objections to a dualistic conception of system and lifeworld also call into question the metaphor of the 'colonization' of the lifeworld by system forces, which has been made popular, but also simplified or even trivialized by some of Habermas's readers and interpreters. This is a powerful picture, of course, that nicely sums up a varied tradition of social criticism that decries the disintegrating effects of commercialization (or 'monetarization') and bureaucratization, alienating occupational roles and compensating consumerism, and the conversion of politically active citizens to dependent welfare clients. The metaphor of 'colonization' also has a certain analytical appeal because it points to a single structural cause of our social troubles. It seems to me, however, that this is an overly generalized and therefore oversimplified diagnosis. I confine myself to the example of legal intervention. In his *Theory of Communicative Action* Habermas diagnosed certain forms of legal intervention (of 'juridification' or 'legalization') as a mode of 'colonization', of undue assimilation of the lifeworld to the structure of the economic and administrative system (Habermas, 1987a: Ch. VIII).

There is a valid idea behind this, of course. The idea is that there are certain forms of social relationship or certain forms of social life and certain types of conflict that are not amenable to legal regulation. The law can fix rights and duties and thereby distribute claims and it can provide for procedures where such claims can be brought forward, and these procedures have by necessity been geared to reaching some definite decision on a limited issue by way of some kind of outside intervention based on public assessment (which requires that a 'case' be made which can be examined by outsiders) and in the end possibly enforced by threat or application of sanctions. The law is by necessity built on the assumption that persons are able to act autonomously and that they have enough skills, knowledge and self-confidence to articulate and defend their claims, to get adequate professional help if necessary and so on. If this is not given (as in legal protection for children), legal conflict regulation also gets into trouble. Also, problems in complex social relationships (for instance, intimate and enduring relationships) can often not really be reduced to definite claims and transparent cases. Outside intervention which is directed at decisions and possibly their enforcement will often not resolve the problems, at least not in the direction of a restoration of relationships. Often the law can at best secure an exit option. Alternative procedures such as mediation relax these requirements somewhat, but only slightly, and they can have other drawbacks. In other words: there are limits to legal intervention (as has been long understood) (Pound, 1916) and variations in the forms of legal intervention or in legal procedure can (for all we know) overcome these constraints only to a certain degree.

However, these considerations hardly allow for a neat distinction between legal interventions which are integrative, and regulations or interventions which are disintegrative. But this is what Habermas initially tried to do. And he even looked for general or formal features of legal regulations themselves, which would distinguish between these two classes.[26] But forms of legal regulation may be appropriate in one case and less so in another. And most often the effects are mixed or ambiguous anyway. His own examples show this best: he refers to family law (especially child custody cases) and legal regulation of schools. But as he himself admits there are reasons for legal intervention in these cases, and it is not at all clear what the alternatives might be (except some notion of judicial restraint and the idea of procedural regulations which should allow the contestants to resolve their conflicts themselves – unfortunately we do not learn how this could be achieved). Neither is it clear whether such forms of social disintegration as family troubles are generally caused by the 'systems' or whether they are really made worse by 'legalization' or 'juridification'.[27] Nor is it clear to me how the tendency of 'juridification' itself might be explained within the framework of 'system' and 'lifeworld'. In short: I do not think the notion of 'colonization' is of much help in analyzing the problems of legal intervention that I have mentioned. What might be helpful, however, would be a closer analysis of forms of social integration and of possible forms of distortion and disintegration, and of possible conflicts or problems of compatibility between different social spheres in modern, highly differentiated societies. Habermas has given a considerable number of valuable leads and analytical instruments for this.

VI Conclusions

My discussion has provided support for some general, important tenets of Professor Habermas's research program. I tried to describe what his conception of 'reconstructive' analysis means, in contrast to other empirical approaches to legal or, more generally, social and cultural phenomena. In particular I tried to clarify the difference between an internal, reconstructive access to symbolic realities and external, 'constructivist' approaches. Another important theoretical tenet is the combination of internal, reconstructive and external, empirical-analytical modes of analysis, which have to be applied to the symbolic and non-symbolic elements and processes within social reality. On the other hand I made some objections: the important analytical distinction between social integration and system integration has sometimes been, but should not be, trivialized as a contrast between a 'living', informal, creative social world and 'mechanical', entirely self-directing social systems. How far are political and legal institutions actually self-directing, separated and independent from other social processes and influences? In which way and to what degree are they internally regulated by non-intentional mechanisms and processes, not by meaningful interactions? These are important empirical questions. Further objections relate to some aspects of Habermas's reconstructive theorizing: normative theorizing and empirical reconstructions of normative contents of cultural belief systems or social institutions should be more clearly kept distinct. There are ambiguities in the way Habermas treats the basic normative principles of modern democratic and constitutional orders: the importance of various substantive normative principles or rights seems too much diminished vis-a-vis procedural norms or process values. These considerations lead to some other important tasks for informed empirical research: the symbolical, normative principles and paradigms which are actually operative in western legal and political systems should be uncovered by more systematic and empirically based analyses. Different modes of discourse should be treated separately and their interrelations assessed: normative political theory (mostly academic discourse), legal and constitutional argument, and public political debates, beliefs and attitudes (in their elitist and more popular versions). Habermas and others have made a case that these symbolic, normative structures should be taken seriously within empirical social research. We have some interesting general considerations and hypotheses. We have also some more specific empirical reconstructions. But in general this kind of work is still very underdeveloped.

Universität Bremen, Germany

On reconstructive legal and political theory

Notes

1 Throughout the text, I refer to this book as *FG*.
2 For finer distinctions see Peters (1991: 33–45).
3 There are of course strong cultural and institutional factors within the social sciences which support such positions. Among them are critical reactions against certain traditional styles of normative or legalistic theorizing in political and legal theory; the influence of scientific ideals borrowed from the natural sciences; a regard for objectivity and 'value neutrality', which often leads to a disregard for the role of normativity within social reality; and a pervasive 'debunking' attitude, often called 'realism', marked by a general distrust in the force of 'ideas' or 'ideals' and a worldly-wise preference for the 'bad man view'.
4 Some of these theories use 'constructivism' as a label themselves; see Knorr-Cetina (1989) for an overview. For 'radical constructivism', cf. Luhmann et al. (1990).
5 For a short (and critical) overview on the new constructivist sociology of science see Harriet Zuckerman's chapter in the *Handbook of Sociology* (Smelser, 1988). Pierre Bourdieu's work, where he analyzes the use of symbolic means in processes of status competition and status reproduction, shares important features of such a theoretical approach.
6 The concept 'social construction of reality' has been made popular, of course, by the seminal book of Berger and Luckmann (1966). Their work represents a unique combination of a phenomenological analysis of structures of consciousness and sociological considerations on processes of routinization and institutionalization. Some of my objections to the 'constructivist' paradigm I would also apply to their work. But I will not discuss their particular blend of analytical approaches here.
7 In the sense that I am using it here, the notion 'reconstructive social science' has been employed by Habermas. Cf. 'Reconstruction and Interpretation in the Social Sciences' in Habermas (1990: 21–42).
8 Much of this systematizing work is very similar to jurisprudential analyses. Following the distinctions between approaches to law which are summarized in Figure 1, jurisprudence as a discipline is a form of practical discourse about law, while reconstruction is not. But the two modes of analysis are certainly overlapping, and reconstructive inquiries into the field of law will always heavily rely on jurisprudential efforts.
9 Of course, these rational explanations must be applied carefully. We should leave room for explanations in the form that people did what they did (or came to change their beliefs) because they had good,

intelligible reasons for this. Nevertheless it can always be asked what contingent circumstances further or hinder such insights. And above all we have to make sure that these rational factors were actually operative, that the good reasons or learning processes that might explain certain developments were actually there. This principle is routinely violated by rational choice theory, which just imputes a model of rational choice to actors without verifying actual process. Conceptions of 'rational reconstruction' in the history of science seem to be based on a similar principle of imputation (Lakatos, 1978). For a formulation of the more empirically based understanding of rational explanation that I have hinted at, see Henderson (1990).

10 Edward Shils aptly expressed this principle some time ago (Shils, 1980: 38).

11 The same argument that purely external theoretical explanations of beliefs or intentional activities involve the theorist in inconsistency or self-contradiction has been made with respect to behaviourisms in psychology (Turner, 1991: 30), to 'cultural materialism' (Westen, 1984: 642), to relativist tendencies in anthropology (Jarvie, 1985: 757) and to a relativist sociology of knowledge (Meynell, 1977: 497–8; Brown, 1989).

12 Ashmore (1989) tries to deal with the paradox by embracing it.

13 For a similar attempt see the work of Klaus Eder, one of Habermas's collaborators (Eder, 1976, 1978).

14 A distinction between the logic of justification and the logic of application has been extensively elaborated by one of Habermas's collaborators, cf. Günther (1988).

15 This is a much abbreviated rendition of his argument in *Faktizität und Geltung*. Habermas's actual argument is much more complex, with many references to philosophical and legal theories, especially from the German tradition, and his presentation of arguments pro-ceeds in a somewhat different order. My account preserves, I think, some essential aspects of his position which are relevant for my discussion.

16 Similar arguments have been made by Manin (1987); Cohen (1989); March and Olsen (1986); Elster (1986; 1991).

17 This is a central normative intuition in Habermas's whole work. Its first elaborate articulation can be found in his important study on the *Structural Transformation of the Public Sphere* (Habermas, 1989a; originally published in German in 1962).

18 Habermas derives this principle on the basis of more fundamental considerations on language, reason and morality, which must not concern us here. Note that this general 'Diskursprinzip' is transformed for purposes of political deliberation within a legal-political

On reconstructive legal and political theory

    community (as distinct from general moral discourse) into the principles of legitimacy which I described above.

19 Habermas treats welfare rights as a special case. He expressly states that these rights (as distinct from other rights and liberties) are only justified insofar as they enable citizens to participate equally in the democratic process (*FG*: 503–4). But do we protect people against misery and starvation only for the reason that we want them to be able to be politically active citizens? The need for safeguards against paternalism (which Habermas has in mind) does not imply such an extremely one-sided justification of welfare rights.

20 This is a transposition of Rawls's distinction between perfect and imperfect, pure and quasi-pure procedural justice. See Rawls (1971: 85–7, 354–66).

21 There may also be important procedural rules of a different, non-institutional sort – namely, rules of argumentation. One example may be rules for the treatment of moral conflicts which cannot be resolved for the time being by rational argument and where recourse to simple bargaining is not appropriate either. For examples see Gutmann and Thompson (1990).

22 Whether this last form of analysis should still be called 'reconstructive' in Habermas's sense is not clear to me. But this is merely a matter of definition. How these forms of 'false consciousness' or distorted communication could themselves be explained I cannot discuss here.

23 This is a somewhat simplified rendition of Habermas's more complex (and sometimes ambiguous) conceptualization; but it brings out the essential point.

24 On the 'embeddedness' of market structures see, for example, Granovetter (1985). On symbolic elements within organizations (private or public) see only the recent 'institutionalist' literature (Powell and DiMaggio, 1991).

25 This parallels the celebration, in some recent political writing, of a 'civil society' which is somehow detached from the 'state' or the institutionalized political sphere, including 'electoral politics', and which is seen, apparently for that reason, as the exclusive locus of collective reason and creativity.

26 Habermas initially tried to make a distinction between 'law as institution' and 'law as medium', based on presumably different forms of legitimation. But he later retracted the idea. One intuition behind this was the idea that there are forms of law which are central for our identity as members of an autonomous citizenry, while other forms have a merely instrumental function. But this does not pertain to the problem of 'juridification'.

27 Habermas also refers to some standard critiques of the 'reifying'

effects of welfare law; to me it seems highly questionable whether this diagnosis is generally correct.

Bibliography

Ashmore, Malcolm (1989) *The Reflexive Thesis*. Chicago, IL: University of Chicago Press.

Berger, Peter and Luckmann, Thomas (1966) *The Social Construction of Reality*. New York: Doubleday.

Black, Donald (1976) *The Behavior of Law*. Orlando, FL: Academic Press.

Blau, Peter M. (1977) *Inequality and Heterogenity: A Primitive Theory of Social Structure*. New York: Free Press.

Blau, Peter M. (1987) 'Contrasting Theoretical Perspectives', in Jeffrey C. Alexander, Bernhard Giesen, Richard Münch and Neil J. Smelser (eds) *The Micro-Macro Link*. Berkeley/Los Angeles: University of California Press.

Brown, James Robert (1989) *The Rational and the Social*. London: Routledge.

Cohen, Joshua (1989) 'Deliberation and Democratic Legitimacy', in Alan Hamlin and Philip Pettit (eds) *The Good Polity. Normative Analysis of the State*. Oxford: Basil Blackwell.

Eder, Klaus (1976) *Die Entstehung staatlich organisierter Gesellschaften*. Frankfurt am Main: Suhrkamp.

Eder, Klaus (1978) 'Zur Rationalisierungsproblematik des modernen Rechts', *Soziale Welt* 29: 247–56.

Elster, Jon (1986) 'The Market and the Forum: Three Varieties of Political Theory', in Jon Elster and A. Hylland (eds) *The Foundations of Social Choice Theory*. Cambridge: Cambridge University Press.

Elster, Jon (1991) 'Arguing and Bargaining in Two Constituent Assemblies'. The Storrs Lectures. Yale Law School.

Friedman, Lawrence M. (1985) *Total Justice*. New York: Russell Sage Foundation.

Friedman, Lawrence M. (1990) *The Republic of Choice: Law, Authority & Culture*. Cambridge, MA: Harvard University Press.

Granovetter, Mark (1985) 'Economic Action and Social Structure: The Problem of Embeddedness', *American Journal of Sociology* 91: 481–510.

Günther, Klaus (1988) *Der Sinn für Angemessenheit. Anwendungsdiskurse in Moral und Recht*. Frankfurt am Main: Suhrkamp.

Gutmann, Amy and Thompson, Dennis (1990) 'Moral Conflict and Political Consensus', *Ethics* 101: 64.

Habermas, Jürgen (1979) *Communication and the Evolution of Society.* Boston, MA: Beacon Press.

Habermas, Jürgen (1984) *The Theory of Communicative Action.* Vol. I, *Reason and the Rationalization of Society.* Boston, MA: Beacon Press.

Habermas, Jürgen (1987a) *The Theory of Communicative Action.* Vol. II, *System and Lifeworld: A Critique of Functionalist Reason.* Boston, MA: Beacon Press.

Habermas, Jürgen (1987b) 'Wie ist Legitimität durch Legalität möglich?' *Kritische Justiz* 20: 1.

Habermas, Jürgen (1988) *Nachmetaphysisches Denken.* Frankfurt am Main: Suhrkamp.

Habermas, Jürgen (1989a) *The Structural Transformation of the Public Sphere: An Inquiry into a Category of Bourgeois Society.* Cambridge, MA: MIT Press.

Habermas, Jürgen (1989b) 'Towards a Communication-Concept of Rational Collective Will-Formation. A Thought-Experiment', *Ratio Juris* 2: 144.

Habermas, Jürgen (1990) *Moral Consciousness and Communicative Action.* Cambridge, MA: MIT Press.

Habermas, Jürgen (1991) *Erläuterungen zur Diskursethik.* Frankfurt am Main: Suhrkamp.

Habermas, Jürgen (1992) *Faktizität und Geltung.* Frankfurt am Main: Suhrkamp.

Henderson, David K. (1990) 'On the Sociology of Science and the Continuing Importance of Epistemological Couched Accounts', *Social Studies of Science* 20: 113.

Holmes, Oliver Wendell Jr (1897) 'The Path of the Law', *Harvard Law Review* 10: 457.

Jarvie, I. C. (1985) 'Anthropology as Science and the Anthropology of Science and of Anthropology or Understanding and Explanation in the Social Sciences, Pt. II', in Peter Asquith and Philip Kitcher (eds) *PSA 1984.* Volume Two. East Lansing, MI: Philosophy of Science Association.

Knorr-Cetina, Karin (1989) 'Spielarten des Konstruktivismus: Einige Notizen und Anmerkungen', *Soziale Welt* 40: 86.

Lakatos, Imre (1978) 'History of Science and Its Rational Reconstructions', in Imre Lakatos, *The Methodology of Scientific Research Programs. Philosophical Papers.* Cambridge: Cambridge University Press.

Luhmann, Niklas (1985) *A Sociological Theory of Law.* London: Routledge & Kegan Paul.

Luhmann, Niklas, et al. (1990) *Beobachter. Konvergenz der Er-kenntnistheorie?* Munich: Wilhelm Fink Verlag.

Manin, Bernard (1987) 'On Legitimacy and Political Deliberation', *Political Theory* 15: 338.

March, James G. and Olsen, Johan P. (1986) 'Popular Sovereignty and the Search for Appropriate Institutions', *Journal of Public Policy* 6: 341.

March, James G. and Olsen, Johan P. (1989) *Rediscovering Institutions. The Organizational Basis of Politics.* New York: Free Press.

Mayhew, Bruce (1980–1) 'Structuralism versus Individualism. Part I: Shadowboxing in the Dark. Part II: Ideological and Other Obfus-cations', *Social Forces* 59: 335, 626.

Meynell, Hugo (1977) 'On the Limits of the Sociology of Knowledge', *Social Studies of Science* 7: 489.

Peters, Bernhard (1991) *Rationalität, Recht und Gesellschaft.* Frankfurt am Main: Suhrkamp.

Post, Robert C. (1986) 'The Social Foundations of Defamation Law: Reputation and the Constitution', *California Law Review* 74: 691.

Post, Robert C. (1988) 'Cultural Heterogeneity and Law: Pornography, Blasphemy and the First Amendment', *California Law Review* 76: 297.

Post, Robert C. (1989) 'The Social Foundations of Privacy Law: Com-munity and Self in the Common Law Tort', *California Law Review* 77.

Post, Robert C. (1990) 'The Constitutional Concept of Public Discourse: Outrageous Opinion, Democratic Deliberation, and *Hustler Maga-zine* v. *Falwell*', *Harvard Law Review* 103: 601.

Pound, Roscoe (1916) 'The Limits of Effective Legal Action', *Inter-national Journal of Ethics* 27: 150–67.

Powell, Walter W. and DiMaggio, Paul, eds (1991) *The New Institutional-ism in Organizational Analysis.* Chicago: University of Chicago Press.

Rawls, John (1971) *A Theory of Justice.* Cambridge, MA: Belknap Press of Harvard University Press.

Scheppele, Kim (1988) *Legal Secrets.* Chicago: University of Chicago Press.

Schluchter, Wolfgang (1979) *Die Entwicklung des okzidentalen Rational-ismus.* Tübingen: Mohr.

Shils, Edward (1975) *Center and Periphery.* Chicago: University of Chicago Press.

Shils, Edward (1980) *The Calling of Sociology and Other Essays on the Pursuit of Learning.* Chicago: University of Chicago Press.

Smelser, Neil J., ed. (1988) *Handbook of Sociology.* Newbury Park, CA: Sage.

Steiner, Henry J. (1987) *Moral Argument and Social Vision in the Courts: A Study of Tort Accident Law*. Madison: University of Wisconsin Press.

Turner, Stephen (1991) 'Social Constructionism and Social Theory', *Sociological Theory* 9: 22.

Westen, Drew (1984) 'Cultural Materialism: Food for Thought or Bum Steer?' *Current Anthropology* 25: 639.

Jürgen Habermas

Postscript to *Between Facts and Norms*

There is a sense in which an author first learns what he has said in a text from the reactions of his readers. In the process he also becomes aware of what he meant to say, and he gains the opportunity to express more clearly what he wanted to say. I find myself in this position hardly one year after the appearance of my book – and after reading an array of intelligent, mainly sympathetic, and in any case instructive reviews. Certainly the interpreter enjoys the advantage of understanding a text better than the author himself; but on the occasion of a new printing the author may be permitted to take the role of an interpreter and attempt to recapitulate the core idea that informs the whole book as he sees it. This also allows him to clear up some of the objections that have been raised in the meantime.

I

Modern law is formed by a system of norms that are coercive, positive and – so it is claimed – freedom-guaranteeing. The formal properties of coercion and positivity are associated with the claim to legitimacy: the fact that norms backed by the threat of state sanction stem from the changeable decisions of a political lawgiver is linked with the expectation that these norms guarantee the autonomy of all legal persons equally. This expectation of legitimacy is intertwined with the facticity of lawmaking and law enforcement. And this connection is in turn mirrored in the ambivalent mode of legal validity. For modern law presents a Janus-face to its addressees: it leaves it up to them which of two possible approaches they want to take to law. They can either

Published by permission of Blackwell Publishers (world excluding North America) and of MIT Press in North America.

consider legal norms merely as commands, in the sense of factual constraints on their personal scope for action, and take a *strategic* approach to the calculable consequences of possible rule violations; or they can take a *performative* attitude in which they view norms as valid precepts and comply 'out of respect for the law'. A legal norm has validity whenever the state guarantees two things at once: on the one hand, the state ensures average compliance, compelled by sanctions if necessary; on the other hand, it guarantees the institutional preconditions for the legitimate genesis of the norm itself, so that it is always at least possible to comply out of respect for the law.

What grounds the legitimacy of rules that can be changed at any time by the political lawgiver? This question becomes especially acute in pluralistic societies in which comprehensive world-views and collectively binding ethics have disintegrated, societies in which the surviving post-traditional morality of conscience no longer supplies a substitute for the natural law that was once grounded in religion or metaphysics. The democratic procedure for the production of law evidently forms the only postmetaphysical source of legitimacy. But what provides this procedure with its legitimating force? Discourse theory answers this question with a simple, and at first glance unlikely, answer: democratic procedure makes it possible for issues and contributions, information and reasons to float freely; it secures a discursive character for political will-formation; and it thereby grounds the fallibilist assumption that results issuing from proper procedure are more or less reasonable. Two considerations provide prima-facie grounds in favor of a discourse-theoretic approach.

From the standpoint of *social theory*, law fulfills socially integrative functions; together with the constitutionally organized political system, law provides a safety net for failures to achieve social integration. It functions as a kind of 'transmission belt' that picks up familiar structures of mutual recognition familiar from face-to-face interactions and transmits these, in an abstract but binding form, to the anonymous, systemically mediated interactions among strangers. Solidarity – the third source of societal integration besides money and administrative power – arises from law only indirectly, of course: by stabilizing behavioral expectations law simultaneously secures symmetrical relationships of reciprocal recognition between abstract bearers of individual rights. These structural similarities between law and communicative action explain why discourses, and thus reflexive forms of communicative action, play a constitutive role for the production (and application) of legal norms.

From the standpoint of *legal theory*, the modern legal order can draw its legitimacy only from the idea of self-determination: citizens should always be able to understand themselves also as authors of the law to which they are subject as addressees. Contractualist theories have construed the autonomy of citizens in the categories of bourgeois contract law, that is, as the private free choice of parties who conclude a contract. But the Hobbesian problem of grounding a social order could not be satisfactorily resolved in terms of the fortuitous confluence of rational choices made by independent actors. This led Kant to equip the parties in the state of nature with genuinely moral capacities, as Rawls would later do with parties in the original position. Today, following the linguistic turn, discourse theory provides an interpretation of this deontological understanding of morality. Consequently, a discursive or deliberative model replaces the contract model: the legal community constitutes itself not by way of a social contract but on the basis of a discursively achieved agreement.

The break with the tradition of rational natural law is incomplete, however, as long as *moral* argumentation remains the exemplar for a constitution-founding discourse. Then, as we find in Kant, the autonomy of citizens coincides with the free will of moral persons, and morality or natural law continues to make up the core of positive law.[1] This model is still based on the natural-law image of a hierarchy of laws: positive law remains subordinate to, and is oriented by, the moral law. In fact, however, the relation between morality and law is much more complicated.

The argument developed in *Faktizität und Geltung* essentially aims to demonstrate that there is a conceptual or internal relation, and not simply an historically contingent association, between the rule of law and democracy. As I have shown in the last chapter, this relation is also evident in the dialectic between legal and factual equality, a dialectic that first called forth the social-welfare paradigm in response to the liberal understanding of law and that today recommends a proceduralist self-understanding of constitutional democracy. The *democratic process* bears the entire burden of legitimation. It must simultaneously secure the private and public autonomy of legal subjects. For individual private rights cannot even be adequately formulated, let alone politically implemented, if those affected have not first engaged in public discussions to clarify which features are relevant in treating typical cases as alike or different, and then mobilized communicative power for the consideration of their newly interpreted needs. The proceduralist understanding of law thus privileges the communicative presuppositions and procedural conditions of democratic opinion- and will-formation as the sole source of legitimation. The proceduralist view is just as incompatible with the platonistic idea that positive law can draw its legitimacy from a higher law as it is with the empiricist denial of any legitimacy beyond the contingency of legislative decisions. To demonstrate an internal relation between the rule of law and democracy, then, we must explain why positive law cannot simply be subordinated to morality (section II); show how popular sovereignty and human rights reciprocally presuppose each other (section III); and make it clear that the principle of democracy has its own roots independent of the moral principle (section IV).

II

1

Certainly morality and law both serve to regulate interpersonal conflicts; and both are supposed to protect the autonomy of all participants and affected persons equally. Interestingly enough, however, the positivity of law forces autonomy to *split up* in a way that has no parallel in morality. Moral self-determination is a unitary concept, according to which each person obeys just those norms that he considers binding according to his own impartial judgment. By contrast, the self-determination of citizens appears in the dual form of private and public autonomy. Legal autonomy does not coincide with freedom in the moral sense. It includes two further moments – the free choice of rationally deciding actors as well as the existential choice of ethically deciding persons.

In the first instance, individual rights have the character of *releasing* legal persons from moral precepts in a carefully circumscribed manner and granting agents the scope for legitimate free choice. With these rights, modern law as a whole upholds the principle that whatever is not explicitly prohibited is permitted. Whereas in morality an inherent symmetry exists between rights and duties, legal *duties* only result as consequences of the protection of *entitlements*, which are conceptually prior. However, private autonomy does not simply mean free choice within legally secure boundaries; it also forms a protective cover for the individual's ethical freedom to pursue his own existential life-project or, in Rawls's words, his current conception of the good.[2] A moral dimension first appears in the autonomy that enfranchised citizens as co-legislators must exercise in common so that everyone can equally enjoy individual liberties. Unlike the moral autonomy that is *equivalent* to the capacity for rational self-binding, then, the autonomy of the legal person includes three different components – besides the jointly exercised autonomy of citizens, the capacities for rational choice and ethical self-realization.

The exercise of legal autonomy divides into the public use of communicative liberties and the private use of individual liberties. This differentiation is explained by the positivity of a law that stems from the collectively binding decisions of lawmaking (and law-applying) agencies. Hence conceptually it requires at least a provisional separation of roles between authors who make (and apply) valid law and addressees who are subject to law. However, if the autonomy of the legal person involves more than autonomy in the moral sense, then positive law cannot be conceived as a special case of morality.

2

Other reasons also preclude a hierarchical conception of natural and positive law. Moral and legal prescriptions each have different reference groups and regulate different matters. The *moral* universe, which is unlimited in social space and historical time, encompasses *all* natural persons in their life-historical complexity. To this extent, it refers to the moral protection of the integrity of fully individuated persons. By contrast, a spatio-temporally localized *legal community* protects the integrity of its members only insofar as they acquire the status of bearers of individual rights.

Morality and law also differ in their extensions. The matters that are in need of, and capable of, legal regulation are at once narrower and broader in scope than morally relevant concerns: they are narrower inasmuch as legal regulation has access only to external, that is, coercible, behavior; and they are broader inasmuch as law, as a means for organizing political rule, provides collective goals or programs with a binding form, and thus is not *exhausted* in the regulation of interpersonal conflicts. Policies and legal programs have a greater or lesser moral weight from case to case, for the matters in need of legal regulation certainly do not raise moral questions *only*, but also involve empirical, pragmatic and ethical aspects, as well as issues concerned with the fair balance of interests open to compromise. Thus the opinion- and will-formation of the democratic legislature depends upon a complicated network of discourses and bargaining – and not simply on moral discourses. And unlike the clearly focused normative validity claim of moral commands, the legitimacy claim of legal norms – like the legislative practice of justification itself – is supported by different types of reasons.[3]

In summary, we can say that law has a more complex structure than morality because it (1) simultaneously unleashes and normatively limits individual freedom of action (with its orientation toward each individual's own values and interests), and (2) incorporates collective goal-setting, so that its regulations are too concrete to be justifiable by moral considerations alone. As an alternative to the natural-law subordination of law to morality, it makes sense to view actionable positive law as a functional complement to morality: it *relieves* the judging and acting person of the considerable cognitive, motivational and – given the moral division of labor often required to fulfill positive duties – organizational demands of a morality centered on the individual's conscience. Law, as it were, compensates for the functional weaknesses of a morality that, from the observer perspective, frequently delivers cognitively indeterminate and motivationally unstable results. This *complementary* relation, however, by no means implies that law enjoys moral neutrality. Indeed, moral reasons enter into law by way of the legislative process. Even if moral considerations are not selective enough for the legitimation of legal programs, politics and law are still supposed to be compatible with morality – on a common postmetaphysical basis of justification.[4]

The doubling of law into natural law and positive law suggests the idea that historical legal orders are supposed to *copy* a pregiven intelligible order. The discourse-theoretic concept of law steers between the twin pitfalls of legal positivism and natural law: if the legitimacy of positive law is conceived as procedural rationality and ultimately traced back to an appropriate communicative arrangement for the lawgiver's rational political will-formation (and for the application of law), then the inviolable moment of legal validity need not disappear in a blind *decisionism* nor be preserved from the vortex of temporality by a moral *containment*. The leading question of modern natural law can then be reformulated under new, discourse-theoretic premises: what rights must citizens mutually grant one another if they decide to constitute themselves as a voluntary association of legal consociates and legitimately to regulate their living together by means of positive law? The performative *meaning* of this constitution-founding practice already contains *in nuce* the entire content of constitutional democracy. The system of rights and the principles of the constitutional state can be developed from what it means to carry out the practice that one has gotten into with the first act in the self-constitution of such a legal community.

If we have to undertake this reconstruction of law without the support of a higher or prior law enjoying moral dignity, then the foregoing considerations lead to two problems: section III raises the question of how we should conceive the equal guarantee of private and public autonomy, if we situate liberty rights, conceived as human rights, in the same dimension of positive law as political rights; section IV confronts us with the question of how we should understand the standard for the legitimacy of law, the discourse principle, if the *complementarity* of law and morality prohibits us from identifying it with the moral principle.

III

The internal relation between the rule of law and democracy can be explained at a conceptual level by the fact that the individual liberties of the subjects of private law and the public autonomy of enfranchised citizens reciprocally make each other possible. In political philosophy this relation is typically presented in such a way that the private autonomy of members of society is guaranteed by human rights (the classical rights to 'life, liberty and property') and an anonymous *rule of law*, while the political autonomy of enfranchised citizens is derived from the principle of popular sovereignty and takes shape in democratic *self-legislation*. In the tradition, however, the relation between these two elements is marked by an unresolved *competition*. The *liberalism* going back to Locke has, at least since the 19th century, invoked the danger of tyrannical majorities and postulated a priority of human rights in relation to popular sovereignty, while the *civic republicanism* reaching back to Aristotle has always granted priority to the political 'liberty of the ancients' over the unpolitical 'liberty of the moderns'. Even Rousseau and Kant missed the intuition they wanted to articulate. Human rights, which for Kant are summarized in the 'original' right to equal individual liberties, must neither be merely imposed on the sovereign legislator as an external constraint nor be instrumentalized as a functional requisite for legislative aims.

Human rights may be quite justifiable as *moral* rights; yet as soon as we conceive them as elements of *positive* law, it is obvious that they cannot be paternalistically imposed on a sovereign legislator. The addressees of law would not be able to understand themselves as its authors if the legislator were to discover human rights as pregiven moral facts that merely need to be enacted as positive law. At the same time, this legislator, regardless of his autonomy, should not be able to adopt anything that violates human rights. For solving this dilemma it now turns out to be an advantage that we have characterized law as a unique kind of medium that is distinguished from morality by its formal properties.

A constitution-founding practice requires more than just a

discourse principle by which citizens can judge whether the law they enact is legitimate. Rather, the very forms of communication that are supposed to make it possible to form a rational political will through discourse need to be legally institutionalized themselves. In assuming a legal shape, the discourse principle is transformed into a principle of democracy. For this purpose, however, the legal code as such must be available, and establishing this code requires the creation of the status of possible legal persons, i.e. of persons who belong to a voluntary association of bearers of actionable individual rights. Without this guarantee of private autonomy, something like positive law cannot exist at all. Consequently, without the classical rights of liberty that secure the private autonomy of legal persons, there is also no *medium* for legally institutionalizing those conditions under which citizens can first make use of their civic autonomy.

Subjects who want to legitimately regulate their living together by means of positive law are no longer free to choose the medium in which they can realize their autonomy. They participate in the production of law only as *legal subjects*; it is no longer in their power to decide which language they will use in this endeavor. Consequently, the desired internal relation between 'human rights' and popular sovereignty consists in the fact that the requirement of legally institutionalizing self-legislation can be fulfilled only with the help of a code that *simultaneously* implies the guarantee of actionable individual liberties. By the same token, the equal distribution of these liberties (and their 'fair value') can in turn only be satisfied by a democratic procedure that grounds the supposition that the outcomes of political opinion- and will-formation are reasonable. This shows how private and public autonomy reciprocally presuppose one another in such a way that neither one may claim primacy over the other.

The critique of liberalism entailed by this idea has roused defenders of the primacy of human rights. Thus Otfried Höffe, for example, has objected to the demotion of *human* rights (whose universal validity he wants to ground anthropologically) to mere *basic legal* rights.[5] If one wants to speak of 'law' only in the sense of positive law, then in fact one must distinguish between *human* rights as morally justified norms of action and human *rights* as positively valid constitutional norms. Such basic [constitutional] rights have a different status from moral norms — norms that may have the same meaning. As enacted, actionable norms, constitutional rights are valid within a particular legal community. But this status does not contradict the universalistic meaning of the classical liberties that include all persons as such and not only all members of a legal community. Even as basic legal rights, they extend to all persons insofar as the latter simply reside within the boundaries of the legal order: to this extent, everyone enjoys the protection of the constitution. In the Federal Republic of Germany, for example, the legal status of aliens, displaced foreigners and stateless persons has at least approached the status of citizens because of the human-rights *meaning* of these basic rights; these groups enjoy the same legal protection and have, according to the letter of the law, similar duties and entitlements.[6]

The discrepancy between, on the one hand, the human-rights content of classical liberties and, on the other, their form as positive law, which initially limits them to a nation-state, is just what makes one aware that the discursively grounded 'system of rights' points beyond the constitutional state in the singular toward the globalization of rights. As Kant realized, basic rights require, by virtue of their semantic content, an international, legally administered 'cosmopolitan society'. For actionable rights to issue from the United Nations Declaration of Human Rights, it is not enough simply to have international courts; such [courts] will first be able to function adequately only when the age of individual sovereign states has come to an end through a United Nations that *can not only pass, but also act upon and enforce its resolutions.*[7]

In defending the primacy of human rights, liberals follow the plausible intuition that legal persons ought to be protected from the state's abuse of its monopoly on violence [*Gewalt*]. Thus Charles Larmore believes that at least *one* individual right – which is morally grounded – has to precede and constrain democratic will-formation: 'No one should be forcibly compelled to submit to norms whose validity cannot be made evident to reason.'[8] On a harmless reading, the argument holds that persons who want to constitute themselves as a legal community have *eo ipso* accepted a concept of positive law that includes the expectation of legitimacy. In that case the need for justification is one of the semantic implications of this concept of law and thus is part of the practice of constitution-founding as such. On a stronger reading, however, the argument expresses the particular belief that the impersonal rule of law is as fundamental as the violence of the Leviathan it is supposed to enchain.

However, this liberal motif, which is explained by obvious historical experiences, does not do justice to the constitutive connection between law and politics.[9] It conflates popular sovereignty with the monopoly on violence and misses the inherently technical, and in any case non-repressive, meaning of an administrative power [*Macht*] appearing in the form of law – insofar as this power is exercised within the framework of democratic laws. Above all, it misses the constitutive meaning that an intersubjectively exercised civic autonomy has for every political community. To do justice to both democratic self-determination and the rule of law requires a two-stage reconstruction. One starts with the horizontal sociation of citizens who, recognizing *one another* as equals, mutually accord rights to one another. Only then does one advance to the constitutional disciplining of the power [*Gewalt*] presupposed with the medium of law. By proceeding in two steps one sees that the liberal rights protecting the individual against the state apparatus with its monopoly on violence are by no means *originary*, but rather emerge from a transformation of individual liberties that were at first *reciprocally* granted. The individual rights linked with the legal code as such acquire only secondarily the negative meaning of delimiting a private sphere that is supposed to be free from arbitrary administrative interference. Rights against the state only arise as a *consequence* of the process of differentiation in which a self-governing association of consociates under law becomes a legal community organized around a state. Such rights arise co-originally with the constitutional principle of legality of administration; hence in the conceptual construction of the system of rights they do not have the fundamental position that Larmore gives them in order to ground the primacy of human rights.

IV

Positive law can no longer derive its legitimacy from a higher ranking moral law, but only from a procedure of presumptively rational opinion- and will-formation. Using a discourse-theoretic approach, I have more closely analyzed this democratic procedure that lends legitimating force to lawmaking under conditions of social and ideological pluralism.[10] In doing so, I started with a principle that I cannot justify here, namely that the only regulations and ways of acting that may claim legitimacy are those to which all who are possibly affected could assent as participants in rational discourses.[11] In the light of this 'discourse principle' citizens test which rights they should mutually accord one another. *As* legal subjects, they must anchor this practice of self-legislation in the medium of law itself; they must legally institutionalize those communicative presuppositions and procedures of a political opinion- and will-formation in which the discourse principle is applied. Thus the establishment of the legal code, which is undertaken with the help of the universal right to equal individual liberties, must be *completed* through communicative and participatory rights that guarantee equal opportunities for the public use of communicative liberties. In this way the discourse principle acquires the legal shape of a democratic principle.

Contrary to what Onora O'Neill seems to assume, here the counterfactual idea that a norm deserves universal assent is by no means absorbed and neutralized by the facticity that attends the legal institutionalization of public discourse.[12] Albrecht Wellmer rightly emphasizes that the

> ... concept of the legitimacy of law also has a *counterfactual* application. Admittedly, it lies within the logic of the modern concept of legitimacy that the common nature of any decisionmaking process must as far as possible be realized *in actual fact* – that is, insofar as all those affected are ultimately to be accorded an equal right to participate in the collective processes by which the common will is formed: this is the idea of democracy. But if legitimate laws are to be such that all those affected would have been capable of passing them collectively, and if all those affected are – in principle – to have an equal right to participate in the collective decisionmaking process, then it goes without saying that the settling of normative questions by means of public argument must play a central part in any attempt to realize the possibility of legitimate law . . . and to ensure that the law is acknowledged as legitimate. To argue in favor of a legal norm – or a system of legal norms – means in this case the attempt to provide reasons which convince all other affected persons why all people of goodwill and discernment should necessarily be able to deem it to be equally in the interests of all that this norm or these norms should prevail in society.[13]

To be sure, this tension between facticity and validity is already built into moral discourse – as it is in the practice of argumentation in general; in the medium of law it is simply intensified and operational-ized.

Wellmer, however, wants to reserve the idea of universal rational acceptability for explaining the legitimacy of *law* and not have it extend to the validity of *moral* norms. He assumes it is a mistake for discourse ethics to carry over the connection between normative validity and real discourse, which is present in the special case of legal validity, to the validity of moral commands. In this context we cannot concern ourselves with this objection itself;[14] but it does draw our attention to a demarcation problem that the discourse theory of law and morality in fact poses. For if, unlike Wellmer, one does not bring in the discourse principle exclusively to explain the principle of democ-racy, but employs it more generally to explicate the meaning of the impartial assessment of normative questions of *every kind*, then one runs the risk of blurring the boundary between the postconventional justification of norms of action in general and the justification of moral norms in particular. In my view, the discourse principle must be situated at a level of abstraction that is still neutral vis-a-vis the distinction between morality and law. On the one hand, it is supposed to have a normative content sufficient for the impartial assessment of norms of action as such; on the other hand, it must not coincide with the moral principle, because it is only subsequently differentiated into the moral principle and the democratic principle. Therefore, it must be shown to what extent the discourse principle does not already exhaust the content of the discourse-ethical principle of universalization (U). Otherwise, the moral principle that was merely concealed in the discourse principle would once again – as in natural law – be the sole source of legitimation in law.

It is important to note that the two key concepts in the proposed formulation of the discourse principle (D) remain indeterminate: 'Only those norms of action are valid to which all possibly affected persons could assent as participants in rational discourses.' This formula does not specify the different 'norms of action' (and corresponding normative statements) or the different 'rational discourses' (on which, incidentally, bargaining depends insofar as its procedures must be discursively justified). This provides enough latitude, however, for deriving the democratic and moral principles by appropriately specifying the discourse principle. Whereas the democratic principle is applied only to norms that display the formal properties of legal norms, the moral principle – according to which valid norms are in the equal interest of all persons[15] – signifies a restriction to the kind of discourse in which *only* moral reasons are decisive. The moral principle does not specify the type of norm, whereas the democratic principle does not specify the forms of argumentation (and bargaining). That explains two asymmetries. Whereas moral discourses are specialized for a single type of reason, and moral norms are furnished with a corresponding mode of normative validity that is sharply focused, the legitimacy of legal norms is supported by a broad spectrum of reasons, including moral reasons. Secondly, whereas the moral principle, as a rule of argument, serves exclusively in the formation of *judgments*, the principle of democracy structures not only knowledge, but, at the same time, the institutional *practice* of citizens.

Note that if one defines the relation between morality and law this way and no longer uses the common label of 'rightness' to identify the legitimacy claim of legal norms with the claim to moral justice,[16] then one can leave open the further question of whether there are *moral* grounds for entering a legal order at all – the problem that rational natural law posed as the transition from the state of nature to civil society. The positive law that we find in modernity as the outcome of a societal learning process has formal properties that recommend it as a suitable instrument for stabilizing behavioral expectations; there does not seem to be any functional equivalent for this in complex societies. Philosophy makes *unnecessary* work for itself when it seeks to demonstrate that it is not simply functionally recommended, but also morally required that we organize our common life by means of positive law, and thus that we form legal communities. The philosopher should be satisfied with the insight that in complex societies, law is the only medium in which it is possible reliably to establish morally obligated relationships of mutual respect even among strangers.

V

Law is not a narcissistically self-enclosed system, but is nourished by the 'democratic *Sittlichkeit* [ethical life]' of enfranchised citizens and a liberal political culture that meets it halfway.[17] This becomes clear when one attempts to explain the paradoxical fact that legitimate law can arise from mere legality. The democratic procedure of lawmaking relies on citizens making use of their communicative and participatory rights *also* with an orientation toward the common good, an attitude that can indeed be politically called for but not legally compelled. Like all individual rights, the form of political rights is also such that they merely grant spheres for free choice and only make legal behavior into a duty. Despite this structure, however, they can open up the sources of legitimation in discursive opinion- and will-formation only if citizens do not exclusively use their communicative liberties *like* individual liberties in the pursuit of personal interests, but rather use them *as* communicative liberties for the purpose of a 'public use of reason'. Law can be preserved as legitimate only if enfranchised citizens switch from the role of private legal subjects and take the perspective of participants who are engaged in the process of reaching understanding about the rules for their life in common. To this extent, constitutional democracy depends on the motivations of a population *accustomed* to liberty, motivations that cannot be generated by administrative measures. This explains why, in the proceduralist paradigm of law, the structures of a vibrant civil society and an unsubverted political public sphere must bear a good portion of the normative expectations, especially the burden of a normatively expected democratic genesis of law.

Not surprisingly, this brings out the skeptic in both the social scientist and the legal scholar. As an empiricist, the former teaches us about powerless ideas that always look foolish in the face of interests; as a pragmatist, the latter teaches us about the hardened conflicts that can only be dealt with by calling upon the backing of a substantial state power. Precisely the discourse-theoretic approach introduces a realistic element insofar as it shifts the conditions for a rational political opinion- and will-formation from the level of *individual* or group motivations and decisions to the *social* level of institutionalized processes of deliberation and decision-making. With this move, a *structuralist* point of view comes into play: democratic procedures and their correspond- ing communicative arrangements can function as a filter that sorts out issues and contributions, information and reasons, in such a way that only the relevant and valid inputs 'count'. Nevertheless, one must still answer the question of how a demanding self-understanding of law that, pace Kant, is not designed for a 'race of devils' is at all compatible with the functional conditions of complex societies.

It was just this skepticism that led me to focus on the tension between facticity and validity in the first place.[18] A reconstructive legal theory follows a methodology premissed on the idea that the counter- factual self-understanding of constitutional democracy finds ex- pression in unavoidable, yet factually efficacious idealizations that are presupposed by the relevant practices. The first act of a constitution- founding practice already inserts an expansive idea into societal complexity like a wedge. In the light of this idea of the self-constitution of a community of free and equal persons, established practices of making, applying and implementing law cannot avoid being exposed to critique and self-critique. In the form of individual rights, the energies of free choice, strategic action and self-realization are simultaneously released and channeled by compelling norms, about which citizens must reach an understanding by following democratic procedures and publicly making use of their legally guaranteed communicative liberties. The paradoxical achievement of law thus consists in the fact that it reduces the conflict potential of unleashed individual liberties through norms that can coerce only so long as they are recognized as legitimate on the fragile basis of unleashed communi- cative liberties. A force that otherwise stands opposed to the socially integrating force of communication is, in the form of legitimate coercion, thus converted into the means of social integration itself. Social integration thereby takes on a peculiarly reflexive shape: by meeting its need for legitimation with the help of the productive force of communication, law takes advantage of a permanent risk of dissensus to spur on legally institutionalized public discourses.

Translated by William Rehg

Notes

Editor's note: page numbers in these notes refer to the German editions of *Faktizität und Geltung* (Frankfurt, Suhrkamp, 1992); a translation of the book is forthcoming from The MIT Press.

1 This interpretation of Kantian private law is contested by I. Maus in *Zur Aufklärung der Demokratietheorie* (Frankfurt, 1992), pp. 148 ff.

2 J. Rawls, *Political Liberalism* (New York, 1992).

3 Political questions are normally so complex that they require the simultaneous treatment of pragmatic, ethical and moral *aspects*. To be sure, these aspects are only *analytically* distinct. Thus my attempt in *Faktizität und Geltung*, Chapter 4, section II.3, pp. 203 ff., to exemplify different types of discourses by ordering concrete questions in a linear fashion is misleading.

4 Naturally, one must distinguish between morally grounded rights and policies; not all legitimate political programs ground rights. Thus, on the one hand, there are strong moral grounds for an individual right to political asylum and a corresponding guarantee of legal remedies (which may not be replaced by institutional guarantees provided by the state). On the other hand, the individual has no absolute legal claim to immigration, although western societies are indeed morally obligated to uphold a liberal immigration policy. In *Faktizität und Geltung*, Appendix II, section III, pp. 658 ff., I have not drawn these distinctions clearly enough; but see my reply to Charles Taylor, 'Struggles for Recognition in Constitutional States', *European Journal of Philosophy* 1 (1993): 128–55.

5 O. Höffe, 'Eine Konversion der Kritischen Theorie?', *Rechtshistorisches Journal* 12 (1993).

6 By this I do not mean to deny the limitations that still exist, especially those deficits in German citizenship law [*Staatsbürgerrechts*], which have been discussed for some time in connection with the issues of foreigners' right to vote in local elections, and 'dual' citizenship, *Faktizität und Geltung*, Appendix II, pp. 653 ff.

7 See the Nachwort to J. Habermas, *Vergangenheit als Zukunft* (Munich, 1993).

8 C. Larmore, 'Die Wurzeln radikaler Demokratie', *Deutsche Zeitschrift für Philosophie* 41 (1993): 327.

9 For the conceptual analysis, see *Faktizität und Geltung*, Chapter 4, section I, pp. 167–87.

10 See pp. 195–207, 369 ff. in *Faktizität und Geltung*.

11 See pp. 138 ff. in *Faktizität und Geltung*. The idea that a norm

deserves universal approval elucidates what it means for norms of action to be valid in terms of a rational acceptability that is not just local. This explication of normative validity pertains to the process of justification, not application, of norms. Thus the comparison with a maxim of judicial decision-making is out of place; see N. Luhmann, 'Quod Omnes Tangit . . .', *Rechtshistorisches Journal* 12 (1993).

12 O. O'Neill, 'Kommunikative Rationalität und praktische Vernunft', *Deutsche Zeitschrift für Philosophie* 41 (1993): 329–32.

13 A. Wellmer, 'Ethics and Dialogue: Elements of Moral Judgement in Kant and Discourse Ethics', in A. Wellmer, *The Persistence of Modernity*, trans. D. Midgley (Cambridge, MA, 1991), p. 194.

14 For my critique of Wellmer, see J. Habermas, *Justification and Application: Remarks on Discourse Ethics*, trans. C. Cronin (Cambridge, MA, 1993), pp. 30 ff; also L. Wingert, *Gemeinsinn und Moral* (Frankfurt am Main, 1993).

15 See the formulation of (U) in J. Habermas, *Moral Consciousness and Communicative Action* (Cambridge, MA, 1990), p. 120: 'For a norm to be valid, the consequences and side-effects that its general observance can be expected to have for the satisfaction of the particular interests of each person affected must be such that all affected can accept them freely.'

16 Cf. R. Alexy, *Begriff und Geltung des Rechts* (Freiburg, 1992).

17 On the concept of democratic *Sittlichkeit*, see A. Wellmer, 'Bedingungen einer demokratischen Kultur', in M. Brumlik and H. Brunkhorst (eds) *Gemeinschaft und Gerechtigkeit* (Frankfurt am Main, 1993), pp. 173–96; also, in the same volume, A. Honneth, 'Posttraditionale Gesellschaften', pp. 260–70.

18 See *Faktizität und Geltung*, Chapter 1, sections III.2–III.3, pp. 53–60.

Mathieu Deflem

Habermas, modernity and law

A bibliography

This bibliography provides a selection of the literature related to Habermas's approach to law, including Habermas's most central writings on the matter. While I have striven for comprehensiveness, certain omissions may no doubt have occurred. The present selection, however, may be a helpful guide to acquaint a broad audience of scholars in legal studies with what has unquestionably grown into a very extensive debate.

The bibliography is divided into two parts. The first section covers the most important writings Jürgen Habermas has devoted to the study of law. I have also added the most significant of Habermas's related texts on politics, democracy and the welfare state, specifically his excursions on current political affairs in united Europe and (re)united Germany. This selection includes German original writings and English translations, which are cross-referenced.

The second section includes secondary writings addressing issues of Habermas's thought on law. To ease entry into this wide-ranging debate, the secondary writings are divided in three parts: (1) general discussions related to Habermas's legal theory, including works which have been influential for the development of Habermas's approach; (2) works that specifically criticize and/or apply Habermas's theory in the field of legal studies; and (3) discussions of Habermas's perspective of discourse ethics in relation to law. On the latter issue, I have in this bibliography retained only writings that discuss themes more narrowly related to law. For additional sources the reader may consult the existing bibliographies on Habermas's moral philosophy; see Michael Zillis, 'Universalism and Communitarianism: A Bibliography', in D. M. Rasmussen (ed.) *Universalism vs. Communitarianism* (Cambridge, MA: The MIT Press, 1990); and the bibliographies in Sheila Benhabib and Fred Dallmayr (eds) *The Communicative Ethics Controversy* (Cambridge, MA: The MIT Press, 1990) and Michael Kelly (ed.) *Hermeneutics and Critical Theory in Ethics and Politics* (Cambridge, MA: The MIT Press, 1990).

1 Habermas on law: primary writings

(1962) *Strukturwandel der Öffentlichkeit: Untersuchungen zu einer Kategorie der bürgerlichen Gesellschaft.* Darmstadt/Neuwied: Hermann Luchterland (English translation: 1989a).

(1963) 'Naturrecht und Revolution.' In J. Habermas, *Theorie und Praxis: Sozialphilosophische Studien.* Neuwied/Berlin: Hermann Luchterland (English translation: 1974).

(1971) 'Theorie der Gesellschaft oder Sozialtechnologie: Eine Auseinandersetzung mit Niklas Luhmann.' In J. Habermas and N. Luhmann, *Theorie der Gesellschaft oder Sozialtechnologie: Was leistet die Systemforschung?* Frankfurt: Suhrkamp.

(1973) *Legitimationsprobleme im Spätkapitalismus.* Frankfurt: Suhrkamp (English translation: 1976c).

(1974) 'Natural Law and Revolution.' In J. Habermas, *Theory and Practice.* London: Heinemann (translation of 1963).

(1976a) 'Zur Rekonstruktion des historischen Materialismus.' In J. Habermas, *Zur Rekonstruktion des historischen Materialismus.* Frankfurt: Suhrkamp (English translation: 1979).

(1976b) 'Überlegungen zum evolutionären Stellenswert des modernen Rechts.' In J. Habermas, *Zur Rekonstruktion des historischen Materialismus.* Frankfurt: Suhrkamp.

(1976c) *Legitimation Crisis.* London: Heinemann Educational Books (translation of 1973).

(1979) 'Toward a Reconstruction of Historical Materialism.' In J. Habermas, *Communication and the Evolution of Society.* London: Heinemann (translation of 1976a).

(1981)*Theorie des kommunikativen Handelns.* Band 1, *Handlungsrationalität und gesellschaftliche Rationalisierung.* Band 2, *Zur Kritik der funktionalistischen Vernunft.* Frankfurt: Suhrkamp (English translation: 1984b, 1987b).

(1983) *Moralbewußtsein und kommunikatives Handeln.* Frankfurt: Suhrkamp (English translation: 1990b).

(1984a) 'Über Moralität und Sittlichkeit: Was macht eine Lebensform "rational"?' In H. Schnädelbach, ed., *Rationalität: Philosophische Beiträge*. Frankfurt: Suhrkamp.

(1984b) *The Theory of Communicative Action*. Volume 1, *Reason and the Rationalization of Society*. Boston: Beacon Press (translation of 1981).

(1985a) *Der philosophische Diskurs der Moderne: Zwölf Vorlesungen*. Frankfurt: Suhrkamp (English translation: 1987c).

(1985b) 'Ziviler Ungehorsam: Testfall für den demokratischen Rechtsstaat.' In J. Habermas, *Die neue Unübersichtlichkeit: Kleine politische Schriften V*. Frankfurt: Suhrkamp (English translation: 1985f).

(1985c) 'Recht und Gewalt: Ein deutsches Trauma.' In J. Habermas, *Die neue Unübersichtlichkeit: Kleine politische Schriften V*. Frankfurt: Suhrkamp (English translation: 1985g).

(1985d) 'Die Krise des Wohlfahrtstaates und die Erschöpfung utopischer Energien.' In J. Habermas, *Die neue Unübersichtlichkeit: Kleine politische Schriften V*. Frankfurt: Suhrkamp (English translation: 1989b).

(1985e) 'Entsorgung der Vergangenheit.' In J. Habermas, *Die neue Unübersichtlichkeit: Kleine politische Schriften V*. Frankfurt: Suhrkamp.

(1985f) 'Civil Disobedience: Litmus Test for the Democratic Constitutional State.' *Berkeley Journal of Sociology* 30: 96–116 (translation of 1985b).

(1985g) 'Right and Violence: A German Trauma.' *Cultural Critique* 1: 125–139 (translation of 1985c).

(1986a) 'Gerechtigkeit und Solidarität: Eine Stellungnahme zur Diskussion über Stufe 6.' In W. Edelstein and G. Nunner-Winkler, eds, *Bestimmung der Moral: Philosophische und sozialwissenschaftliche Beiträge zur Moralforschung*. Frankfurt: Suhrkamp (English translation: 1990k).

(1986b) 'Moralität und Sittlichkeit: Treffen Hegels Einwände gegen Kant auch auf die Diskursethik zu?' In W. Kuhlman, ed., *Moralität und Sittlichkeit: Das Problem Hegels und die Diskursethik*. Frankfurt: Suhrkamp (English translation: 1990b).

(1987a) 'Wie ist Legitimität durch Legalität möglich?' *Kritische Justiz* 20: 1–16 (English translation: 1988).

(1987b) *The Theory of Communicative Action*. Volume 2, *System and Lifeworld: A Critique of Functionalist Reason*. Boston: Beacon Press (translation of 1981).

(1987c) *The Philosophical Discourse of Modernity: Twelve Lectures*. Cambridge: Polity Press (translation of 1985a).

(1987d) 'Keine Normalisierung der Vergangenheit.' In J. Habermas, *Eine Art Schadensabwicklung: Kleine politische Schriften VI.* Frankfurt: Suhrkamp.

(1987e) 'Über den doppelten Boden des demokratischen Rechtsstaates.' In J. Habermas, *Eine Art Schadensabwicklung: Kleine politische Schriften VI.* Frankfurt: Suhrkamp.

(1987f) 'Über Moral, Recht, zivilen Ungehorsam und Moderne.' In J. Habermas, *Eine Art Schadensabwicklung: Kleine politische Schriften VI.* Frankfurt: Suhrkamp (English translation: 1992f).

(1987g) 'Eine Art Schadensabwicklung' [four essays]. In J. Habermas, *Eine Art Schadensabwicklung: Kleine politische Schriften VI.* Frankfurt: Suhrkamp (English translation: 1989e).

(1987h) 'Geschichtsbewußtsein und posttraditionale Identität: Die Westorientierung der Bundesrepublik.' In J. Habermas, *Eine Art Schadensabwicklung: Kleine politische Schriften VI.* Frankfurt: Suhrkamp (English translation: 1989f).

(1988) 'Law and Morality.' In S. M. McMurrin, ed., *The Tanner Lectures on Human Values.* Volume 8. Salt Lake City: University of Utah Press (includes translation of 1987a).

(1989a) *The Structural Transformation of the Public Sphere: An Inquiry into a Category of Bourgeois Society.* Cambridge, MA: The MIT Press (translation of 1962).

(1989b) 'The New Obscurity: The Crisis of the Welfare State and the Exhaustion of Utopian Energies.' In J. Habermas, *The New Conservatism: Cultural Criticism and the Historians' Debate.* Cambridge, MA: The MIT Press (translation of 1985d).

(1989c) 'Political Culture in Germany since 1968: An Interview with Dr Rainer Erd for the *Frankfurter Rundschau*.' In J. Habermas, *The New Conservatism: Cultural Criticism and the Historians' Debate.* Cambridge, MA: The MIT Press.

(1989d) 'The New Intimacy between Culture and Politics: Theses on Enlightenment in Germany.' In J. Habermas, *The New Conservatism: Cultural Criticism and the Historians' Debate.* Cambridge, MA: The MIT Press (German version in 1990c).

(1989e) 'A Kind of Settling Damages' [four essays]. In J. Habermas, *The New Conservatism: Cultural Criticism and the Historians' Debate.* Cambridge, MA: The MIT Press (translation of 1987g).

(1989f) 'Historical Consciousness and Post-Traditional Identity: The Federal Republic's Orientation to the West.' In J. Habermas, *The New Conservatism: Cultural Criticism and the Historians' Debate.* Cambridge, MA: The MIT Press (translation of 1987h).

(1989g) 'Towards a Communication-Concept of Rational Collective Will-Formation: A Thought-Experiment.' *Ratio Juris* 2: 144–154.

(1989h) 'Der Philosoph als wahrer Rechtslehrer: Rudolf Wiethölter.' *Kritische Justiz* 22: 138–146.

(1990a)*Vergangenheit als Zukunft* [interviews, edited by M. Haller]. Zürich: Pendo-Verlag.

(1990b) *Moral Consciousness and Communicative Action.* Cambridge, MA: The MIT Press (translation of 1983, including 1986b).

(1990c) 'Die neue Intimität zwischen Kultur und Politik.' In J. Habermas, *Die nachholende Revolution: Kleine politische Schriften VII.* Frankfurt: Suhrkamp (English translation: 1989d).

(1990d) 'Interview mit T. Hviid Nielsen.' In J. Habermas, *Die nachholende Revolution: Kleine politische Schriften VII.* Frankfurt: Suhrkamp (English translation: 1990j, 1993a).

(1990e) 'Grenzen des Heohistorismus' [interview]. In J. Habermas, *Die nachholende Revolution: Kleine politische Schriften VII.* Frankfurt: Suhrkamp (English translation: 1990l).

(1990f) 'Die Stunde der nationalen Empfindung: Republikanische Gesinnung oder Nationalbewußtsein?' In J. Habermas, *Die nachholende Revolution: Kleine politische Schriften VII.* Frankfurt: Suhrkamp.

(1990g) 'Gewaltmonopol, Rechtsbewußtsein und demokratischer Prozeß: Erste Eindrücke bei der Lektüre des "Entgutachtens" der Gewaltkommission.' In J. Habermas, *Die nachholende Revolution: Kleine politische Schriften VII.* Frankfurt: Suhrkamp.

(1990h) 'Nachholende Revolution und linker Revisionsbedarf: Was heißt Sozialismus heute?' In J. Habermas, *Die nachholende Revolution: Kleine politische Schriften VII.* Frankfurt: Suhrkamp (English translation: 1990n).

(1990i) 'Nochmals: Zur Identität der Deutschen: Ein einig Volk von aufgebrachten Wirtschaftsbürgern?' In J. Habermas, *Die nachholende Revolution: Kleine politische Schriften VII.* Frankfurt: Suhrkamp (English translation: 1991b).

(1990j) 'Morality, Society and Ethics: An Interview with Torben Hviid Nielsen.' *Acta Sociologica* 33: 93–114 (translation of 1990d).

(1990k) 'Justice and Solidarity: On the Discussion Concerning Stage 6.' In M. Kelly, ed., *Hermeneutics and Critical Theory in Ethics and Politics.* Cambridge, MA: The MIT Press (translation of 1986a).

(1990l) 'Ethics, Politics and History' [interview with Jean-Marc Ferry]. In D. M. Rasmussen, ed., *Universalism vs. Communitarianism.* Cambridge, MA: The MIT Press (translation of 1990e).

(1990m) 'Remarks on the Discussion.' *Theory, Culture and Society* 7: 127–132.

(1990n) 'What Does Socialism Mean Today? The Rectifying Revolution and the Need for New Thinking on the Left.' *New Left Review* 183: 3–21 (translation of 1990h).

(1991a) *Erläuterungen zur Diskursethik.* Frankfurt: Suhrkamp (includes reprints of 1984a, 1986a, 1986b; English translation: 1993a).

(1991b) 'Yet Again: German Identity: A Unified Nation of Angry DM-Burghers?' *New German Critique* 52: 84–101 (translation of 1990i).

(1992a) *Faktizität und Geltung: Beiträge zur Diskurstheorie des Rechts und des demokratischen Rechtsstaats.* Frankfurt: Suhrkamp (includes German versions of 1988 and 1992d; English translation: forthcoming).

(1992b) 'Bemerkungen zu einer verworrenen Diskussion: Was bedeutet "Aufarbeitung der Vergangenheit" heute?' *Die Zeit* (April 3): 82.

(1992c) 'Die zweite Lebenslüge der Bundesrepublik: Wir sind wieder "normal" geworden.' *Die Zeit* (December 11) 48 (English translation: 1993b).

(1992d) 'Citizenship and National Identity: Some Reflections on the Future of Europe.' *Praxis International* 12: 1–19 (German version in 1992a).

(1992e) 'Further Reflections on the Public Sphere.' In C. Calhoun, ed., *Habermas and the Public Sphere.* Cambridge, MA: The MIT Press.

(1992f) 'On Morality, Law, Civil Disobedience and Modernity.' In P. Dews, ed., *Autonomy and Solidarity: Interviews with Jürgen Habermas* (revised edition). London: Verso (translation of 1987f).

(1993a) *Justification and Application: Remarks on Discourse Ethics.* Cambridge, MA: The MIT Press (translation of 1991a, including 1990d).

(1993b) 'The Second Life Fiction of the Federal Republic: We Have Become "Normal" Again.' *New Left Review* 197: 58–66 (translation of 1992c).

(1993c) [with Adam Michnik] 'Mehr Demut, weniger Illusionen' [interview with Adam Krzeminski]. *Die Zeit* (December 24): 6–8 (English translation: 1994a, 1994b).

(1993d) 'Nachwort.' In Charles Taylor, *Multikulturalismus und die Politik der Anerkennung.* Frankfurt: Suhrkamp.

(1993e) 'Die Asyldebatte.' In J. Habermas, *Vergangenheit als Zukunft: Das Alte Deutschland im neuen Europa?* München: Piper.

(1993f) 'Nachwort.' In J. Habermas, *Vergangenheit als Zukunft: Das Alte Deutschland im neuen Europa?* München: Piper.

(1994a) 'Nachwort (zur vierten, durchgesehenen und um ein Literaturverzeichnis ergänzten Auflage).' In J. Habermas, *Faktizität und Geltung: Beiträge zur Diskurstheorie des Rechts und des demokratischen Rechtsstaats* [fourth edition]. Frankfurt: Suhrkamp (English translation in this issue).

(1994b) [with Adam Michnik] 'Overcoming the Past' [interview with

Adam Krzeminski]. *New Left Review* (203): 3–16 (translation of 1993c).

(1994c) [with Adam Michnik] 'More Humility, Fewer Illusions' [Interview with Adam Krzeminski], *New York Review of Books* 61(6): 24–29 (translation of 1993c).

(1994d) 'Human Rights and Popular Sovereignty: The Liberal and Republican Versions.' *Ratio Juris* 7: 1–13 (translation of pp. 124–135 in 1992a).

(forthcoming) *Between Facts and Norms*. Cambridge, MA: The MIT Press (translation of 1992a).

2 Secondary writings on Habermas and law

2.1 General discussions

Alexy, Robert (1978) *Theorie der juristischen Argumentation: Die Theorie des rationalen Diskurses als Theorie der juristischen Begründigung*. Frankfurt: Suhrkamp (English translation: *A Theory of Legal Argumentation*. Oxford: Clarendon Press, 1989).

Alexy, Robert (1981) 'Die Idee einer prozeduralen Theorie der juristischen Argumentation.' In A. Aarnio, I. Niiniluoto and L. Uusitalo, eds, *Methodologie und Erkenntnistheorie der juristischen Argumentation*. Berlin: Duncker & Humbolt.

Alexy, Robert (1986) *Theorie der Grundrechte*. Frankfurt: Suhrkamp.

Alexy, Robert (1987) 'Rechtssystem und Praktische Vernunft.' *Rechtstheorie* 18: 405–419.

Alexy, Robert (1989) 'On Necessary Relations Between Law and Morality.' *Ratio Juris* 2: 167–183.

Alexy, Robert (1990) 'Problems of Discursive Rationality in Law.' In W. Maihofer and G. Sprenger, eds, *Law and the States in Modern Times*. Stuttgart: Franz Steiner.

Alexy, Robert (1992) *Begriff und Geltung des Rechts*. Freiburg: Campus.

Bal, Peter (1988) *Dwangkommunikatie in de Rechtszaal*. Arnhem: Gouda Quint.

Bal, Peter (1990) 'Procedurele Rationaliteit en Mensenrechten in het Strafproces.' *Recht en Kritiek* 16: 259–279.

Baratta, Alessandro (1991) 'Les Fonctions Instrumentales et les Fonctions Symboliques du Droit Pénal.' *Déviance et Société* 15: 1–25.

Baratta, Alessandro and Silbernagel, Michel (1988) 'Neue Legitimationsstrategien des Strafrechts und ihre Kritik als Realitätskritik.' *Kriminologisches Journal* 20: 32–49.

Blankenburg, Erhard (1984) 'The Poverty of Evolutionism: A Critique of

Teubner's Case for "Reflexive Law".' *Law and Society Review* 18: 273–289.

Böckenförde, E. W. (1991) *Recht, Staat, Freiheit*. Frankfurt: Suhrkamp.

Calhoun, Craig (1989) 'Social Theory and the Law: Systems Theory, Normative Justification, and Postmodernism.' *Northwestern University Law Review* 83: 398–460.

de Haan, Willem (1988) 'The Necessity of Punishment in a Just Social Order.' *International Journal of the Sociology of Law* 16: 433–453.

de Haan, Willem (1990) *The Politics of Redress: Crime, Punishment and Penal Abolition*. London: Allen & Unwin.

Dwars, Ingrid (1992) 'Application Discourse and the Special Case-Thesis.' *Ratio Juris* 5: 67–78.

Dworkin, Ronald (1977) *Taking Rights Seriously*. Cambridge, MA: Harvard University Press.

Dworkin, Ronald (1986) *Law's Empire*. Cambridge, MA: Harvard University Press.

Eder, Klaus (1986) 'Prozedurale Rationalität: Moderne Rechtsentwicklung jenseits von formaler Rationalisierung.' *Zeitschrift für Rechtssoziologie* 7: 1–30.

Eder, Klaus (1987) 'Die Authorität des Rechts: Eine soziale Kritik prozeduraler Rationalität.' *Zeitschrift für Rechtssoziologie* 8: 193–230.

Fish, Stanley (1990) *Doing What Comes Naturally: Change, Rhetoric and the Practice of Theory in Literary and Legal Studies*. Durham: Duke University Press.

Frankenberg, Günther (1989) 'Down by Law: Irony, Seriousness, and Reason.' In C. Joerges and D. M. Trubek, eds, *Critical Legal Thought: An American-German Debate*. Baden-Baden: Nomos.

Günther, Klaus (1988) *Der Sinn für Angemessenheit: Anwendungsdiskurse in Moral und Recht*. Frankfurt: Suhrkamp (English translation: *The Sense of Appropriateness*. Albany, NY: SUNY Press, forthcoming).

Günther, Klaus (1989a) 'Ein normativer Begriff der Kohärenz für eine Theorie der juristischen Argumentation.' *Rechtstheorie* 20: 163–190.

Günther, Klaus (1989b) 'A Normative Conception of Coherence for a Discursive Theory of Legal Justification.' *Ratio Juris* 2: 155–166.

Günther, Klaus (1993) 'Critical Remarks on Robert Alexy's "Special-Case Thesis".' *Ratio Juris* 6: 143–156.

Handler, Joel S. (1990) *Law and the Search for Community*. Philadelphia: University of Pennsylvania Press.

Harden, Ian and Lewis, Norman (1986) *The Noble Lie: The British Constitution and the Rule of Law*. London: Hutchinson.

Heller, Agnes (1987) *Beyond Justice*. New York: Basil Blackwell.

Hoy, David C. (1985) 'Interpreting the Law: Hermeneutical and Poststructuralist Perspectives.' *Southern California Law Review* 58: 135–176.

Husson, Christine A. Desan (1986) 'Expanding the Legal Vocabulary: The Challenge Posed by the Deconstruction and Defense of Law.' *Yale Law Journal* 95: 969–991.

Lilly, J. Robert and Deflem, Mathieu (1993) 'Penologie en Profijt: Een Exploratief Onderzoek naar de Bestraffingsindustrie.' *Delikt & Delinkwent* 23: 511–527.

Lübbe, Weyma (1993) 'Wie ist Legitimität durch Legalität möglich? Rekonstruktion der Antwort Max Webers.' *Archiv für Rechts- und Sozialphilosophie* 70: 80–90.

Luhmann, Niklas (1981) *Ausdifferenzierung des Rechts.* Frankfurt: Suhrkamp.

Luhmann, Niklas (1983a) *Rechtssoziologie.* Opladen: Westdeutscher Verlag (English translation: *A Sociological Theory of Law.* London: Routledge & Kegan Paul, 1985).

Luhmann, Niklas (1983b) *Legitimation durch Verfahren.* Frankfurt: Suhrkamp.

Luhmann, Niklas (1992) 'Operational Closure and Structural Coupling: The Differentiation of the Legal System.' *Cardozo Law Review* 13: 1419–1441.

Luhmann, Niklas (1993) 'The Code of the Moral.' *Cardozo Law Review* 14: 995–1009.

McCahery, Joseph (1993) 'Modernist and Postmodernist Perspectives on Public Law in British Critical Legal Studies.' *Social & Legal Studies* 2: 397–421.

MacIntyre, Alasdair (1981) *After Virtue.* London: Duckworth.

MacIntyre, Alasdair (1988) *Whose Justice? Which Rationality?* Notre Dame: University of Notre Dame.

Maus, Ingeborg (1986) *Rechtstheorie und politische Theorie im Industriekapitalismus.* München: Wilhelm Fink.

Maus, Ingeborg (1992) *Zur Aufklärung der Demokratietheorie.* Frankfurt: Suhrkamp.

Muguerza, Javier (1989) 'The Alternative of Dissent.' In G. B. Peterson, ed., *The Tanner Lectures on Human Values,* Volume 10. Salt Lake City: University of Utah Press.

Mullen, T. (1986) 'Constitutional Protection of Human Rights.' In T. Campbell, D. Goldberg, S. McLean and T. Mullen, eds, *Human Rights: From Rhetoric to Reality.* Oxford: Basil Blackwell.

Munger, Frank and Seon, Carroll (1984) 'Critical Legal Studies versus Critical Legal Theory: A Comment on Method.' *Law & Policy* 6: 257–297.

Nelken, David (1982) 'Is There a Crisis in Law and Legal Ideology?' *Journal of Law and Society* 9: 177–189.

Paulson, Stanley L. (1990) 'Läßt sich die reine Rechtslehre transzendental begründen?' *Rechtstheorie* 21: 155–179.

Peters, Bernhard (1991) *Rationalität, Recht und Gesellschaft*. Frankfurt: Suhrkamp.

Phillips, Derek L. (1986) *Toward a Just Social Order*. Princeton: Princeton University Press.

Preuss, Ulrich K. (1989) 'Rationality Potentials of Law: Allocative, Distributive and Communicative Rationality.' In C. Joerges and D. M. Trubek, eds, *Critical Legal Thought: An American-German Debate*. Baden-Baden: Nomos.

Rawls, John (1971) *A Theory of Justice*. Cambridge, MA: Harvard University Press.

Rawls, John (1985) 'Justice as Fairness: Political not Metaphysical.' *Philosophy and Public Affairs* 14: 223–251.

Rawls, John (1992) *Political Liberalism*. New York.

Röhl, Klaus F. (1993) 'Verfahrensgerechtigkeit (Procedural Justice).' *Zeitschrift für Rechtssoziologie* 14: 1–34.

Teubner, Günther (1983) 'Substantive and Reflexive Elements in Modern Law.' *Law and Society Review* 17: 239–285.

Teubner, Günther (1984) 'Autopoiesis in Law and Society: A Rejoinder to Blankenburg.' *Law and Society Review* 18: 291–301.

Teubner, Günther (1989a) *Recht als autopoietisches System*. Frankfurt: Suhrkamp. (English translation: *Law as an Autopoietic System*. Oxford: Blackwell, 1993.)

Teubner, Günther (1989b) 'How the Law Thinks: Toward a Constructivist Epistemology of Law.' *Law and Society Review* 23: 727–757.

Tushnet, Mark (1988) 'Comment on Eder.' *Law and Society Review* 22: 945–948.

Uusitalo, Liisa (1989) 'Efficiency, Effectiveness and Legitimation: Criteria for the Evaluation of Norms.' *Ratio Juris* 2: 194–201.

Young, Iris M. (1981) 'Toward a Critical Theory of Justice.' *Social Theory and Practice* 7: 279–302.

2.2 Criticisms and applications

Bal, Peter and Ippel, Pieter (1982) 'Waarheen met het Strafrecht? Met Habermas op Weg.' *Recht en Kritiek* 8: 434–462.

Benhabib, Seyla (1982) 'The Methodological Illusions of Political Theory: The Case of Rawls and Habermas.' *Neue Hefte für Philosophie* 21: 47–74.

Bertilsson, Margareta (1994) [review of J. Habermas, *Faktizität und Geltung*]. *Contemporary Sociology* 23: 156–159.

Borucka-Arctowa, Maria (1991) 'Le Role de la Compétence à la Communication: L'Expérience Franco-Polonaise de Socialisation Juridique.' *Droit et Société* 19: 277–286.

Brand, Arie (1987) 'Ethical Rationalization and "Juridification": Habermas' Critical Legal Theory.' *Australian Journal of Law and Society* 4: 103–127.

Cobben, Paul (1989) 'Kan Legitimiteit zuiver Procedureel Gegarandeerd Worden? Een Kritische Beschouwing over Habermas' Conceptie van de Verhouding tussen Moraal, Recht en Politiek.' *Recht en Kritiek* 15: 262–279.

Cobben, Paul (1991) 'De Rechtstheorie van Jürgen Habermas: Ontwikkeling en Receptie.' *Rechtsfilosofie en Rechtstheorie* 20: 107–123.

Cole, David (1985) 'Getting There: Reflections on Trashing from Feminist Jurisprudence and Critical Theory.' *Harvard Women's Law Journal* 8: 59–91.

Dan-Cohen, Meir (1989) 'Law, Community, and Communication.' *Duke Law Journal* 6: 1654–1676.

Deflem, Mathieu (1992a) 'Jürgen Habermas: Pflegevater oder Sorgenkind der abolitionistischen Perspektive.' *Kriminologisches Journal* 24: 330–351.

Deflem, Mathieu (1992b) 'De Communicatie-Theoretische Benadering van het Recht: Fundamenten en Kritieken van de Rechtssociologie van Jürgen Habermas.' *Recht en Kritiek* 18: 235–258.

Deflem, Mathieu (1994) 'La Notion de Droit dans la Théorie de L'Agir Communicationelle de Jürgen Habermas.' *Déviance et Société* 18: 95–120.

Dews, Peter (1993a) 'Faktizität, Geltung und Öffentlichkeit.' *Deutsche Zeitschrift für Philosophie* 2: 359–364.

Dews, Peter (1993b) 'Agreeing What's Right' [review of J. Habermas, *Faktizität und Geltung*]. *London Review of Books* 15: 26–27.

Eder, Klaus (1988) 'Critique of Habermas's Contribution to the Sociology of Law.' *Law and Society Review* 22: 931–944.

Feldman, Stephen M. (1993) 'The Persistence of Power and the Struggle for Dialogic Standards in Postmodern Constitutional Jurisprudence: Michelman, Habermas, and Civic Republicanism.' *Georgetown Law Journal* 81: 2243–2290.

Felts, Arthur A. and Fields, Charles B. (1988) 'Technical and Symbolic Reasoning: An Application of Habermas' Ideological Analysis to the Legal Arena.' *Quarterly Journal of Ideology* 12: 1–15.

Guibentif, Pierre (1989) 'Et Habermas? Le Droit dans l'Oeuvre de Jürgen Habermas: Éléments d'Orientation.' *Droit et Société* 11/12: 159–189.

Haarscher, Guy (1986) 'Perelman and Habermas.' *Law and Philosophy* 5: 331–342.

Höffe, Otfried (1993) 'Eine Konversion der Kritischen Theorie?' *Rechtshistorisches Journal* (12).

Horster, Detlef (1992) 'Jürgen Habermas' Rechtsphilosophie' [review of J. Habermas, *Faktizität und Geltung*]. *Die neue Gesellschaft: Frankfurter Hefte* 39: 1138–1141.

Horster, Detlef (1993) [review of J. Habermas, *Faktizität und Geltung*]. *Archiv für Rechts- und Sozialphilosophie* 79: 588–591.

Ingram, David (1990) 'Dworkin, Habermas, and the CLS Movement on Moral Criticism in Law.' *Philosophy and Social Criticism* 16: 237–268.

Larmore, Charles (1993) 'Die Wurzeln radikaler Demokratie.' *Deutsche Zeitschrift für Philosophie* 2: 321–327.

Leedes, Gary C. (1991) 'The Discourse Ethics Alternative to Rust v. Sullivan.' *University of Richmond Law Review* 26: 87–143.

Luhmann, Niklas (1971) 'Systemtheoretische Argumentationen: Eine Entgegnung auf Jürgen Habermas.' In J. Habermas and N. Luhmann, *Theorie der Gesellschaft oder Sozialtechnologie: Was Leistet die Systemforschung?* Frankfurt: Suhrkamp.

Luhmann, Niklas (1993) 'Quod Omnes Tangit . . .' *Rechtshistorisches Journal* 12: 36–56.

Mehring, Reinhard (1993) 'Legitimität durch kommunikative Verfahren?' [review of J. Habermas, *Faktizität und Geltung*]. *Philosophischer Literaturanzeiger* 46: 172–188.

Melkevik, Bjarne (1990) 'Le Modèle Communicationnel en Science Juridique: Habermas et le Droit.' *Cahiers de Droit* 31: 901–915.

Melkevik, Bjarne (1992) 'Transformation du Droit: Le Point de Vue du Modèle Communicationnel.' *Cahiers de Droit* 33: 115–139.

Merkel, Reinhard (1993) 'Was ist das Recht?' [review of J. Habermas, *Faktizität und Geltung*]. *Die Zeit* (February 12): 57.

Mootz, Francis J. (1988) 'The Ontological Basis of Legal Hermeneutics: A Proposed Model of Inquiry Based on the Work of Gadamer, Habermas, and Ricoeur.' *Boston University Law Review* 68: 523–617.

Murphy, W. T. (1989) 'The Habermas Effect: Critical Theory and Academic Law.' *Current Legal Problems* 42: 135–165.

Northey, Rod (1988) 'Conflicting Principles of Canadian Environmental Reform: Trubek and Habermas v. Law and Economics and the Law Reform Commission.' *Dalhousie Law Journal* 11: 639–662.

O'Neill, Onora (1993) 'Kommunikative Rationalität und praktische Vernunft.' *Deutsche Zeitschrift für Philosophie* 2: 329–332.

Orts, Eric W. (1993) 'Positive Law and Systemic Legitimacy: A Comment on Hart and Habermas.' *Ratio Juris* 6: 245–278.

Pettit, Philip (1982) 'Habermas on Truth and Justice.' In G. H. R. Parkinson, ed., *Marx and Marxisms*. Cambridge: Cambridge University Press.

Raes, Koen (1985) 'Kommunikatief Handelen en Juridisering.' *Recht en Kritiek* 11: 114–150.

Raes, Koen (1986) 'Legalisation, Communication and Strategy: A Critique of Habermas' Approach to Law.' *Journal of Law and Society* 13: 183–206.

Rasmussen, David M. (1988) 'Communication Theory and the Critique of the Law: Habermas and Unger on the Law.' *Praxis International* 8: 155–170.

Rasmussen, David M. (1990) 'Communication and the Law.' In D. M. Rasmussen, *Reading Habermas*. Oxford: Basil Blackwell.

Scheuerman, Bill (1993) 'Neumann v. Habermas: The Frankfurt School and the Case of the Rule of Law.' *Praxis International* 13: 50–67.

Siep, Ludwig (1992) 'Mit Radikalen vernünftig Reden?' [review of J. Habermas, *Faktizität und Geltung*]. *Der Spiegel* 43: 292–298.

Solum, Lawrence B. (1989) 'Freedom of Communicative Action: A Theory of the First Amendment Freedom of Speech.' *Northwestern University Law Review* 83: 54–135.

Somek, Alexander (1993) 'Unbestimmtheit: Habermas und die Critical Legal Studies. Einige Bemerkungen über die Funktion von Rechtsparadigmen für die Rechtsanwendung im demokratischen Rechtsstaat.' *Deutsche Zeitschrift für Philosophie* 2: 343–357.

Sumner, Colin (1983) 'Law, Legitimation and the Advanced Capitalist State: The Jurisprudence and Social Theory of Jürgen Habermas.' In D. Sugerman, ed., *Legality, Ideology and the State*. London: Academic Press.

Tietz, Udo (1993) 'Faktizität, Geltung und Demokratie: Bemerkungen zu Habermas' Diskurstheorie der Wahrheit und der Normenbegründung.' *Deutsche Zeitschrift für Philosophie* 2: 333–342.

Vandenberghe, Frédéric (1993) 'Contra-Facticiteit en Geldigheid: De Staat van de Discussie' [review of J. Habermas, *Faktizität und Geltung*]. *Krisis* 51: 76–79.

Van den Brink, Bert, et al. (1993) 'Jürgen Habermas en de (Duitse) Rechtsstaat.' [Special issue on *Faktizität und Geltung*]. *Filosofie Magazine* 2: 15–24.

Van der Burg, Wibren (1985) 'De Rechtstheorie van Jürgen Habermas.' *Recht en Kritiek* 11: 6–26.

Van der Burg, Wibren (1990) 'Jürgen Habermas on Law and Morality: Some Critical Comments.' *Theory, Culture and Society* 7: 105–111.

Wiggers, J. H. (1987) 'Contract en Rede: Hegel, Rawls en Habermas over de Grondslag van de Politieke Filosofie.' *Rechtsfilosofie en Rechts-theorie* 16: 47–70.

2.3 Discourse ethics and law

Alexy, Robert (1992) 'A Discourse-Theoretical Conception of Practical Reason.' *Ratio Juris* 5: 231–251.

Alexy, Robert (1993) 'Justification and Application of Norms.' *Ratio Juris* 6: 157–170.

Andersen, Hans (1990) 'Morality in Three Social Theories: Parsons, Analytical Marxism and Habermas.' *Acta Sociologica* 33: 321–339.

Apel, Karl-Otto (1988) *Diskurs und Verantwortung: Das Problem des Übergangs zur postkonventionellen Moral.* Frankfurt: Suhrkamp.

Apel, Karl-Otto and Kettner, Matthias (1992, eds) *Zur Anwendung der Diskursethik in Politik, Recht und Wissenschaft.* Frankfurt: Suhrkamp.

Baynes, Kenneth (1991) *The Normative Grounds of Social Criticism: Kant, Rawls and Habermas.* Albany, NY: State University of New York Press.

Belliotti, Raymond A. (1989) 'Radical Politics and Nonfoundational Morality.' *International Philosophical Quarterly* 29: 33.

Benhabib, Seyla and Dallmayr, Fred (1990, eds) *The Communicative Ethics Controversy.* Cambridge, MA: The MIT Press.

Braun, Carl (1988) 'Diskurstheoretische Normenbegründung in der Rechtswissenschaft.' *Rechtstheorie* 19: 238–261.

Calhoun, Craig (1992, ed.) *Habermas and the Public Sphere.* Cambridge, MA: The MIT Press.

Cohen, Jean L. (1988) 'Discourse Ethics and Civil Society.' *Philosophy and Social Criticism* 14: 315–337.

Cohen, Jean L. and Arato, Andrew (1992) *Civil Society and Political Theory.* Cambridge, MA: The MIT Press.

Cortina, Adela (1990) 'Diskursethik und Menschenrechte.' *Archiv für Rechts- und Sozialphilosophie* 76: 37–49.

Donahue, Michael E. and Felts, Arthur A. (1993) 'Police Ethics: A Critical Perspective.' *Journal of Criminal Justice* 21: 339–352.

Ferrara, Alessandro (1985) 'A Critique of Habermas' *Diskursethik.*' *Telos* 64: 45–74.

Ferry, Jean-Marc (1993) 'Une Approche Philosophique de la Rationalité Juridique.' *Droits* 18: 89–98.

Gebauer, Richard (1993) *Letzte Begründung: Eine Kritik der Diskur-sethik von Jürgen Habermas.* München: Wilhelm Fink Verlag.

Günther, Klaus (1990) 'Impartial Application of Moral and Legal Norms: A Contribution to Discourse Ethics.' In D. M. Rasmussen, ed.,

Universalism vs. Communitarianism: Contemporary Debates in Ethics. Cambridge, MA: The MIT Press.

Günther, Klaus (1991) 'Möglichkeiten einer diskursethischen Begründung des Strafrechts.' In H. Jung, H. Müller-Dietz and U. Neumann, eds, *Recht und Moral*. Baden-Baden: Nomos.

Günther, Klaus (1992) 'Universalistische Normenbegründung und Normenwendung in Recht und Moral.' In M. Herberger, U. Neumann and H. Rüssmann, eds, *Individualisierung und Generalisierung im Rechtsdenken*. Stuttgart: Steiner.

Heller, Agnes (1984–85) 'The Discourse Ethics of Habermas: Critique and Appraisal.' *Thesis Eleven* 10/11: 5–17.

Honneth, Axel (1986) 'Diskursethik und implizites Gerechtigkeitskonzept.' In W. Kuhlmann, ed., *Moralität und Sittlichkeit*. Frankfurt: Suhrkamp.

Honneth, Axel, McCarthy, Thomas, Offe, Claus and Wellmer, Albrecht (1992a, eds) *Philosophical Interventions in the Unfinished Project of Enlightenment*. Cambridge, MA: The MIT Press.

Honneth, Axel, McCarthy, Thomas, Offe, Claus and Wellmer, Albrecht (1992b, eds) *Cultural-Political Interventions in the Unfinished Project of Enlightenment*. Cambridge, MA: The MIT Press.

Horster, Detlef (1990) 'Erkenntnis und Moral bei Habermas.' In O. Negt et al., *Theorie und Praxis Heute: Ein Kolloquium zur Theorie und politischen Wirksamkeit von Jürgen Habermas*. Frankfurt: Materialis.

Ingram, David (1993) 'The Limits and Possibilities of Communicative Ethics for Democratic Theory.' *Political Theory* 21: 294–321.

Kelly, Michael (1990a, ed.) *Hermeneutics and Critical Theory in Ethics and Politics*. Cambridge, MA: The MIT Press.

Kelly, Michael (1990b) 'MacIntyre, Habermas and Philosophical Ethics.' In M. Kelly, ed., *Hermeneutics and Critical Theory in Ethics and Politics*. Cambridge, MA: The MIT Press.

Ketschelt, H. (1980) 'Moralisches Argumentieren und Sozialtheorie: Prozedurale Ethik bei John Rawls und Jürgen Habermas.' *Archiv für Rechts- und Sozialphilosophie* 66: 391–429.

Ladrière, Paul (1990) 'De l'Expérience Éthique à une Éthique de la Discussion.' *Cahiers Internationaux de Sociologie* 37: 43–68.

McCarthy, Thomas (1992) 'Practical Discourse: On the Relation of Morality to Politics.' In G. Calhoun, ed., *Habermas and the Public Sphere*. Cambridge, MA: The MIT Press.

Matustik, Martin J. (1993) *Postnational Identity: Critical Theory and Existential Philosophy in Habermas, Kierkegaard and Havel*. New York: Guilford Press.

Mirchandani, Rehka (1992) 'Habermas, Discourse Ethics, and Assuring the Moral Point of View.' *Current Perspectives in Social Theory* 12: 231–249.

Nolte, Helmut (1984) 'Kommunikative Kompetenz und Leibapriori: Zur philosophischen Anthropologie von Jürgen Habermas und Karl-Otto Apel.' *Archiv für Rechts- und Sozialphilosophie* 70: 518–539.

Raffel, Stanley (1992) *Habermas, Lyotard and the Concept of Justice.* London: Macmillan.

Rasmussen, David M. (1990, ed.) *Universalism vs. Communitarianism: Contemporary Debates in Ethics.* Cambridge, MA: The MIT Press.

Rehg, William (1990) 'Discourse Ethics and the Communitarian Critique of Neo-Kantianism.' *Philosophical Forum* 22: 120–138.

Rehg, William (1991) 'Discourse and the Moral Point of View: Deriving a Dialogical Principle of Universalization.' *Inquiry* 34: 27–48.

Rehg, William (1994) *Insight and Solidarity: The Discourse Ethics of Jürgen Habermas.* Berkeley, CA: University of California Press.

Shelley, Robert (1993) 'Habermas and the Normative Foundations of a Radical Politics.' *Thesis Eleven* 35: 62–83.

Torpey, John (1986) 'Ethics and Critical Theory: From Horkheimer to Habermas.' *Telos* 69: 68–84.

Trey, G. A. (1992) 'Communicative Ethics in the Face of Alterity: Habermas, Levinas and the Problem of Post-Conventional Universalism.' *Praxis International* 11: 412–427.

Tuori, Kaarlo (1989a) 'Legitimität des modernen Rechts.' *Rechtstheorie* 20: 221–243.

Tuori, Kaarlo (1989b) 'Discourse Ethics and the Legitimacy of Law.' *Ratio Juris* 2: 125–143.

Wren, T. E. (1990, ed.) *The Moral Domain: Essays in the Ongoing Discussion Between Philosophy and the Social Sciences.* Cambridge, MA: The MIT Press.

3 Appendix: the debate on *Faktizität und Geltung (Between Facts and Norms)*

In the relatively short period since the publication of *Faktizität und Geltung* in 1992, Habermas's innovative theory of law and democracy has already provoked much debate and commentary. This Appendix lists recently published discussions of Habermas's approach and relevant writings by Habermas.

Abraham, David (1994) 'Persistent Facts and Compelling Norms: Liberal Capitalism, Democratic Socialism, and the Law.' *Law & Society Review* 28: 939–946.

Alexy, Robert (1994) 'Basic Rights and Democracy in Jürgen Habermas's Procedural Paradigm of the Law.' *Ratio Juris* 7: 227–238.

Andersen, Heine (1994) 'Jürgen Habermas: *Faktizität und Geltung*' [review article]. *Acta Sociologica* 37: 93–99.

Angerhn, Emil (1993) 'Das unvollendete Projekt der Demokratie' [review of J. Habermas, *Faktizität und Geltung*]. *Philosophische Rundschau* 40: 257–264.

Baynes, Kenneth (1995) 'Democracy and the *Rechtsstaat*: Habermas's *Faktizität und Geltung*.' In S. K. White, ed., *The Cambridge Companion to Foucault*. New York: Cambridge University Press.

Bohman, James (1994) 'Complexity, Pluralism, and the Constitutional State: On Habermas's *Faktizität und Geltung*' [review article]. *Law & Society Review* 28: 897–930.

Casebeer, Kenneth (1994) 'Paris Is Closer than Frankfurt: The *n*th American Exceptionalism.' *Law & Society Review* 28: 931–937.

Deflem, Mathieu (1994) 'Social Control and the Theory of Communicative Action.' *International Journal of the Sociology of Law* 22: 355–373.

Deflem, Mathieu (1995) 'Corruption, Law, and Justice: A Conceptual Clarification.' *Journal of Criminal Justice* 23: 243–258.

Dworkin, Ronald (1995) 'Constitutionalism and Democracy.' *European Journal of Philosophy* 3: 2–11.

Gosepath, Stefan (1995) 'The Place of Equality in Habermas' and Dworkin's Theories of Justice.' *European Journal of Philosophy* 3: 21–35.

Günther, Klaus (1995) 'Legal Adjudication and Democracy: Some Remarks on Dworkin and Habermas.' *European Journal of Philosophy* 3: 36–54.

Habermas, Jürgen (1994a) *The Past as Future*. Lincoln, NE: University of Nebraska Press (translation of *Vergangenheit als Zukunft*, München, Piper, 1991/1993).

Habermas, Jürgen (1994b) 'Burdens of the Double Past.' *Dissent* (Fall): 513–517.

Habermas, Jürgen (1994c) 'Three Normative Models of Democracy.' *Constellations* 1: 1–10.

Habermas, Jürgen (1995a) 'Reconciliation through the Public Use of Reason: Remarks on John Rawls's Political Liberalism.' *Journal of Philosophy* 92: 109–131.

Habermas, Jürgen (1995b) 'Multiculturalism and the Liberal State.' *Stanford Law Review* 47: 849–853 (translation of excerpts from *Faktizität und Geltung*).

Habermas, Jürgen (1995c) 'On the Internal Relation between the Rule of

Law and Democracy.' *European Journal of Philosophy* 3: 12–20 (translation of excerpts from *Faktizität und Geltung*).

Habermas, Jürgen (1995d) 'Interrélations entre Etat de Droit et Democratie.' *Revue Suisse de Sociologie* 21: 11–20 (French translation of 1995c).

Hilgendorf, Eric (1994) 'Rechtsphilosophie im vereinigten Deutschland' [review of J. Habermas, *Faktizität und Geltung*]. *Philosophische Revue* 40: 1ff.

Infomation Philosophie (1993) 'Das diskurstheoretische Rechts- und Demokratiekonzept von Jürgen Habermas' [review of J. Habermas, *Fakizität und Geltung*]. *Information Philosophie* 21: 68–80.

Larmore, Charles (1995) 'The Foundations of Modern Democracy: Reflections on Jürgen Habermas.' *European Journal of Philosophy* 3: 55–68.

McCarthy, Thomas (1994) 'Kantian Constructivism and Reconstructivism: Rawls and Habermas in Dialogue.' *Ethics* 105: 44–63.

Minogue, Kenneth (1994) 'Special Issue: "Habermas, Modernity and Law,"' *Philosophy and Social Criticism*, vol. 20, no. 4' [review article]. *The Times Literary Supplement* (25 November): 27–28.

Outhwaite, William (1994) 'J. Habermas, *Faktizität und Geltung*' [review article]. *Sociology* 28: 340–342.

Peters, Bernhard (1993) *Die Integration moderner Gesellschaften*. Frankfurt: Suhrkamp.

Preyer, Gerhard (1993) 'J. Habermas, *Faktizität und Geltung*' [review article]. *Kölner Zeitschrift für Soziologie und Sozialpsychologie* 45: 373–376.

Rawls, John (1995) 'Reply to Habermas.' *Journal of Philosophy* 92: 132–180.

Schlink, Bernhard (1993) 'Abenddämerung oder Morgendämmerung? Zu Jürgen Habermas' Diskurstheorie des demokratischen Rechtsstaats.' *Rechtshistorisches Journal* 12: 57–69.

Schönberger, Christoph (1994) 'J. Habermas, *Faktizität und Geltung*' [review article]. *Der Staat* (1994): 124–128.

Simon, Jonathan (1994) 'Between Power and Knowledge: Habermas, Foucault, and the Future of Legal Studies.' *Law & Society Review* 28: 947–961.

Tönnies, Sybille (1993) 'J. Habermas, *Faktizität und Geltung*' [review article]. *Rechtstheorie* 24: 387–392.

Tweedy, John & Hunt, Alan (1994) 'The Future of the Welfare State and Social Rights: Reflections on Habermas.' *Journal of Law and Society* 21: 288–316.

Weinberger, Ota (1994) 'Habermas on Democracy and Justice: Limits of a Sound Conception.' *Ratio Juris* 7: 239–253.

Williams, H. (1994) 'Democracy and Right in Habermas's Theory of Facticity and Value' [review of J. Habermas, *Faktizität und Geltung*]. *History of Political Thought* 15: 269ff.

Index